I OVERCAME MY AUTISM AND ALL I GOT WAS
THIS LOUSY ANXIETY DISORDER

SARAH KURCHAK

I Overcame My Autism

AND ALL I GOT WAS THIS LOUSY ANXIETY DISORDER

A MEMOIR

 Douglas & McIntyre

Douglas and McIntyre (2013) Ltd.
P.O. Box 219, Madeira Park, BC, VON 2HO
www.douglas-mcintyre.com

Pillow Fight League photos at top of page vii by Chris Blanchenot. All other
    photos courtesy of the Kurchak family.
Edited by Pam Robertson
Cover design by Anna Comfort O'Keeffe
Text design by Brianna Cerkiewicz
Dingbat designed by Freepik
Printed and bound in Canada
Printed on 100% recycled paper

Douglas and McIntyre (2013) Ltd. acknowledges the support of the Canada
Council for the Arts, the Government of Canada, and the Province of British
Columbia through the BC Arts Council.

Library and Archives Canada Cataloguing in Publication

Title: I overcame my autism and all I got was this lousy anxiety disorder : a
    memoir / Sarah Kurchak.

Names: Kurchak, Sarah, 1982- author.

Identifiers: Canadiana (print) 20190232234 | Canadiana (ebook) 20190232277
    | ISBN 9781771622462 (softcover) | ISBN 9781771622479 (HTML)

Subjects: LCSH: Kurchak, Sarah, 1982- | LCSH: Autistic people—Canada—
    Biography. | LCGFT: Autobiographies.

Classification: LCC RC553.A88 K87 2020 | DDC 616.89/820092—dc23

To Ethel, George, Isobel and Ted
(I think you all knew how desperately I wanted to do this
when you were still around to see it. I know you didn't
need to see it to be proud of me.)

CONTENTS

DISCLAIMER

SO...[1]

I do not speak for all autistic people. I will not try to. I do not want to. I wish to be *a* voice/face of autism in a much greater, more nuanced and diverse conversation, not *the* voice or face of autism.

I don't think that autism is easy. I do not think that it's just a quirk. I'm not arguing for greater acceptance of and support for autistic people because I think that autism is not a big deal. I'm asking for those things because I know it can be a very big deal, indeed. And that, if it is a big deal to me, it is probably a big or bigger deal to many other autistic people.

It is true that I have certain advantages in life that many autistic people do not. I can speak. Some people think that I can write. I have low support needs. People who point out

....

1 No matter how clear—or how repetitive—I try to make myself whenever I try to offer *a* perspective on autism, people will appear and tell me that I do not and cannot offer *the* perspective on autism. Often, these readers—often but not always non-autistic parents of autistic children—will make other assumptions about my work. Few are rooted in anything I've actually attempted to say.

Years of going through this routine has led me to develop an increasingly defensive writing style. It's no longer enough for me to state what I want to say in my work. I must now state what I am not, in any way, trying to say. It's never quite enough to keep the You Don't Speak for All Autistics at bay, but that doesn't stop me from trying.

Apparently an entire book riddled with "I'm not saying ___. I'm just saying ___" gets a bit repetitive, though. So my publisher and editor have helpfully suggested that I write this disclaimer instead.

that these advantages will influence how I experience autism and the world aren't wrong. But I would argue that they don't go far enough. I believe that it's also important to acknowledge that I'm white and cisgender. Race, gender, class, sexuality and disability can influence autistic people's lives and perspectives every bit as much as our support needs do.

While I realize that the world treats me differently than many of my fellow autistic people, I do not think I am better than any other autistic person. And I will always push back against any suggestion that I am.

I am constantly thinking about the diversity of autistic people when I write. I am aware of—or at least constantly working on expanding my understanding of—the limits of my perspective and desperately want to be respectful of that. I don't make many sweeping statements about all autistic people. When I say "many autistic people" or "some autistic people" I mean many or some. Because we are all different. And I can't speak for everyone.

The only thing I will say about all autistic people is that we are all human beings and deserve to be treated as such. Everything else is as different and complicated and nuanced as we are.

While I don't want to presume that I can or should speak for all autistic people, though, I don't want to assume that I can't offer any other autistic people anything, either. There are similarities in many of our experiences as well as differences. I want to offer perspectives and insights that might be of some use to other autistic people. And I have at least some evidence that I can do that. Autistic people of many different support needs, races, genders, sexualities and circumstances have told me that my work has some value for them. I think about that when I write, too.

I do not speak for all autistic people. I will not try to. I do not want to. I wish to be *a* voice/face of autism in a much greater, more nuanced, and diverse conversation, not *the* voice or face of autism.

To anyone who might be suspicious of my motives or my qualifications to write about autism at all: I do not speak *for* all autistic people. I will not try to. I do not want to. This is always on my mind when I'm writing. But many autistic people of different identities and different support needs have told me that I speak *to* them. Please keep this in your mind while you're reading.

To my fellow autistic people and our allies: I do not want to speak for you or over you. I have done my best to use my story as a means of highlighting bigger issues and discussions in our world. Please take what you can use from it. Please know that I say none of this to absolve myself from the limitations and possible failures of what I have written. I know it's not enough. I know one voice never can be. I just hope it's something.

INTRODUCTION

IN 2017, I WROTE AN ESSAY.

This probably shouldn't be remarkable. Certainly not worthy of its own sentence at the beginning of a book introduction. I wrote *an* essay in 2017? Big deal. I wrote fifteen in the following two years, which you're now holding in your hands. It's what I'm supposed to do, being a writer and all. But every essay feels like a perverse miracle that leaches out of me fully formed, like those terrifying snowsuit-clad rage babies sprung from Nola Carveth in David Cronenberg's 1979 body horror classic *The Brood*. I come away from each one having no idea how I managed to accomplish it. I go into the next one having gained absolutely no knowledge or confidence from the experience.

This particular essay was worse. On the surface it was, like most things I was writing at the time, about autism. For me, though, it was about failure and letting go. My life and career were at an impasse. I was lucky to have enough paying work to (barely) sustain me, and grateful that some of it appeared to be meaningful to my fellow autistic people. But I was becoming exponentially more frustrated with the limitations of writing about autism for a largely non-autistic audience—in a medium almost entirely by and for non-autistic people—with each passing assignment. Autistic people were learning more about autism from our own lives and each other, but our outside audience wasn't developing at the same rate.

I was faring all right with basic Autism 101 material: how we feel about the anti-vaccine movement, the state of media representation, how we feel about the anti-vaccine movement, why we don't like eye contact, how some awareness campaigns miss the mark and how we feel about the anti-vaccine movement. Efforts to express something deeper, more nuanced or simply more interesting than that—in words or in life—were generally met with well-meaning but patronizing rejection. This essay was going to be my way of coming to terms with my professional and personal frustrations as best I could. A last gasp of effort in the face of inevitable defeat, like Robert Vaughn's character summoning his final shred of courage before his scenery-chewing death in *The Magnificent Seven*, or legendary wrestler Kazuchika Okada declaring that "a man stands like this, with his hands on a wall, when things are easy in his life" before collapsing into said wall during a backstage interview for the G1 Climax 28. A way to say goodbye to the hopes I'd had for my words and their impact before resigning myself to a lifetime of vaccine op-eds and awkward misunderstandings.

After much crying, pouting and prostrating, this dying light rage baby was published in *Hazlitt* in the middle of Autism Awareness Month 2018:

Real Autism

After years of threatening to write an autistic teen sex comedy based on my own neurodivergent and sexually frustrated adolescence, I had the opportunity to receive notes on a few chapters from an agent. I furtively sent off a chunk of my first draft filled with observations on what it's like to have a seizure in the middle of sex ed and the ways in which an inability to read social cues hampers one's ability to lose their virginity on schedule. He told me that it was "very REAL but also pretty raw." The criticism I could handle. It was, undeniably, raw, in the way that most first drafts are. It was his compliment, sitting there on the screen in its assured, emphatic capital letters, that threw me.

A week later, a fellow mixed martial arts writer reached out to tell me that he liked a piece that I'd written on the late MMA fighter Kimbo Slice's importance to autistic people. A "really amazing and real read," he said. The praise wasn't any more appealing when it appeared in lower case letters.

Like many people with my neurotype, I have a certain affinity for recognizing patterns, and here's one that I've found: no one ever said that my writing was "real" before I knew that I was autistic, or before I started writing about my autism.

Despite the commonly held beliefs about the autistic mind, I am perfectly capable of seeing outside of my own perspective. I know full well that that this is not a phenomenon unique to me or those like me. Another pattern that I've noticed while observing other people—like white rock critics assessing hip hop, men explaining women to themselves or Torontonians who once visited Thailand debating the ketchup content of pad Thai—is that people who aren't marginalized love appointing themselves the authenticity police of those who are, often with a passion and confidence that's inversely proportional to their actual knowledge.

There is something about the word "real," though, that hits me specifically hard as an autistic human.

As a child, it was the crux of my recurring nightmares, awful, bone-chilling romps through a developing psyche that I can still recall in lurid detail. In the dreams, I was a copy that my parents had been forced to take in when the actual Sarah had died. I would try to forget this fact, but there was always some little detail that would come rushing back to me to ruin the illusion. "I remember that," I would say each time, usually before I woke up crying, "from when I was real."

These dreams came up when I was finally tested for autism spectrum disorder as an adult. "You were beginning to realize that you were different, but you didn't understand how yet," my assessor told me as he confirmed a diagnosis that my terrified subconscious had apparently picked up on almost a quarter of a century earlier. "This was your brain's way of trying to process that information."

I processed all of *this* new information with a mix of perverse pride in and a motherly protectiveness for my younger self—*What twisted genius comes up with something like that? What scared little girl has to?*—and a life-giving amount of relief. Weight had been lifted off my shoulders, my chest and my brain simultaneously. I was autistic. I saw, heard, tasted, smelled and interacted with things differently than other people, but I was human. Atypical, but real.

Where I saw the first irrefutable proof of myself, though, so many others saw a referendum.

"But you're not *really* autistic," an acquaintance posited a few weeks later, when I was still testing out how and whether to introduce this new explanation for everything into casual conversation. "You can have conversations. You're out at a bar. I have a friend who's autistic. Like, real autistic. You can tell. And he could never do this." He took my wandering eyes and distracted response as signs of concession, not as a testament to my at least somewhat obvious autism, and moved on. I soon got used to this type of exchange. I'm still hoping that I'll eventually get better at handling it.

I spent twenty-seven years trying to convince people that I was normal enough to accept, or at least leave alone, and no one ever fully bought it. When I finally knew why that experiment was such an ongoing failure, though, few believed that either. I was using it as an excuse. I was exaggerating. I was faking. I was not as autistic as someone else someone knew and was, therefore, not really autistic.

These comparisons only ever go in one direction. No one has ever said to me, "Temple Grandin is a successful scientist, writer and public speaker, and you have the career of a mildly plucky freelancer half your age. You can't possibly be autistic." I suspect that this is because no one is genuinely trying to weigh what they know about me against a set of diagnostic criteria, or fit me into their greater understanding of autistics in the world. What people are really doing when they're trying to determine if I'm really autistic is figuring out if I make them uncomfortable or sad enough to count. If I show any coping skills, any empathy, any likability, any fun—essentially any humanity—I complicate the narrative too much and usually end up ignored.

This separation between real autistics and people who are "just quirky," "just awkward" or "almost too high-functioning to count" is a mental dance that non-autistics have to do whenever they're confronted with a 3-D autistic human being in the flesh. Otherwise everything they've ever thought, everything they've ever been told about us, starts to seem a little monstrous.

In *NeuroTribes: The Legacy of Autism and the Future of Neurodiversity*, the groundbreaking 2015 tome on the subject, author Steve Silberman quotes an interview that Ivar Lovaas gave to *Psychology Today* in the seventies. "You have a person in the physical sense," the clinical psychologist said of the autistic children that he was studying. "But they are not people in the psychological sense."

Few are willing to put it so boldly now, but despite the efforts of artists, self-advocates and allies like Silberman, the philosophy remains almost unchanged and unchallenged forty years later. From common language to science to pop culture, there's very little evidence that suggests anyone believes autistic people are real people at all.

I see it in the way we're described as trapped in our own bodies, as prisoners of capital-A Autism, an otherworldly evil that has kidnapped us and stolen our voices like a cackling Disney villain. It's in the way that the organizations that claim to support us insist on imagery that compares us to wayward jigsaw puzzle pieces and language that alludes to us as the bringers of an overwhelmingly tragic epidemic, yet also somehow missing. One 2015 report warned of a "tsunami of teens with autism" who would reach adulthood in the coming years. It's in both the name and the ethos of our most prominent charity, Autism Speaks, which assumes that we can't do so for ourselves and therefore appoints itself the saviour who can and should assume the responsibility, without any thought as to whether they should be listening, as well.

The missing can't be reached for comment. The voiceless have no means with which to express themselves. The not-really-theres have no internal life to share, anyway. So no one tries.

In science, we are glorified lab rats, put through byzantine tasks to determine why we do certain things—one recent study involved putting autistic adults through virtual reality scenarios in which they tried to catch burglars to figure out why we have issues with eye contact—but not simply asked what makes us tick. The idea that we should be considered a valuable resource for research about our own lives is still a groundbreaking one. In journalism, we are rarely considered prospective sources for stories about autism, in any capacity. Experts are quoted, as are our caregivers. But we remain absent from the conversation. First-person accounts of parents and siblings are praised for their honesty, bravery and emotion while autistic writers struggle to get published at all. The entertainment business has a similar fondness for stories about us and distaste for stories from us. Visionaries can dream up a franchise where an autistic man can be an accountant and a hitman on the screen, like in *The Accountant*, but they can't quite bring themselves to imagine that an autistic person could be a writer, director, actor ... or even a viewer who might want to see something that's made with them in mind.

When people tell me that I'm not really autistic, they're trying to distance me from this silencing, exclusion and dehumanization. Not for my comfort, but theirs. They don't want to weigh the reality of our interaction against the concept of autism that they've accepted. And even if they can convince themselves that it's different for people like me, people who can talk, people who can assuage feelings of discomfort by hiding their behaviours and trying to blend in, I know my own reality. Whatever advantages I might have as a verbal human being with a handy batch of coping and masking mechanisms in place, I am no better than anyone else on the spectrum. We are equals. When I say that autistic lives have value, I'm speaking for every single one of them. When other people imply the opposite about any single one of us, they imply it about all of us.

As a teenager, my nightmares about being a hollow spectre trying to pass as human eventually gave way to fantasies of being an otherworldly genius. Perhaps no one understood me, I thought, because I was simply too complex and too smart. I spent a lot of time reading James Joyce alone in my room and promising myself that I'd grow up to be the kind of writer who makes their readers work to understand their dense prose, heady concepts and labyrinths of allusions and metaphors. Now that I've spent so much of my life working to be acknowledged at all—moving, sounding and performing in a manner that won't push people away before they can hear me—now that I understand what an immense privilege it is to have anyone want to put the effort into understanding you, now that my tiny writing career has given me an opportunity that's denied to most people like me, I try to write plainly.

It's not an aesthetic or career decision that I regret often. After all of the massive, ongoing efforts that I've put into translating myself for non-autistic consumption, I doubt that I know any other way now, anyway. Although I feel the occasional pang of self-consciousness and self-recrimination when someone praises me for the simplicity or accessibility of my writing. Does it mean that my writing is simple? Does that mean that I am? But at least they're reading my work. And there's a solid chance that they're getting some of what I intended out of it.

When someone who's not autistic tells me that my writing is real, though, it chills and confuses me almost as much as those first subconscious stabs at defining the validity of my existence once did. I might try to pass it off with a flippant "How would you know?" But the question that lingers in the back of my mind is: *What makes them think they know?* If almost everything they know about autism is wrong, or at least skewed, then what is it about my work that has allowed them to feel that they can align my voice with their beliefs? Did the basic structure of my prose strike them as special needs enough to accept? Did a moment of vulnerability convince them that I was tragic enough to actually be from the spectrum? Or was I too placating in my argument? Can they embrace my work—can they feel comfortable in telling me what it means—because I haven't challenged them enough?

For as long as autistic narratives are dominated and controlled by others, these are the concerns that will fester in the pit of my stomach and the back of my brain every time I sit down at my laptop, start to rock from side to side, and write.

I have no interest in being told that my writing is real. I need my work to tell you that *I* am.

What I saw as a literary obituary, one agent saw as a call to answer. After reading the essay, she reached out and asked me what kind of book I'd want to write if I were given the opportunity.

I pled my case for the aforementioned autistic teen sex comedy. Then I tried to introduce the novella about Plato, Socrates, professional wrestling and homoerotic fanfiction I'd written in my early twenties into the conversation. To paraphrase Wayne Gretzky, you miss 100 percent of the shots to sell your repurposed adolescent ancient Greek philosopher slash to a bona fide literary agent that you don't take. When she deftly shepherded the conversation toward nonfiction, I mentioned a third dream project: *I Overcame My Autism and All I Got Was This Lousy Anxiety Disorder*. Not a straightforward memoir—no one who has spent a statistically significant portion of their life alone in their room should be allowed to inflict one of those on the world—but a loosely connected series of personal essays that tackled topics important to autistic people and my personal experiences with them. The content was more of an abstract concept at that point, but I was very excited about the title. I signed with her and began working on a book proposal immediately. It was one of those overnight successes almost two decades in the making.

Although I was riding a momentary high on account of the whole fairy god-agent situation, I still wanted to tell my story as a cautionary tale. It's how I genuinely view my life, but this opportunity also gave me a chance to be the change in terms of autism narratives I wanted to see in the world. Most of the stories you hear about autistic people in media and art are either miserable tragedies or inspirational triumphs, while most of our real lives exist somewhere in between. With my book, I could finally introduce some much needed ¯_(ツ)_/¯ into the conversation. Here are some things that accidentally ruined my life. Here are some other things that surprisingly saved it. And here I am, living a neutral autistic life that requires little pity but probably shouldn't be the object of aspiration, either.

When it came time to figure out how I was going to loosely thread those suckers together, the only thing that made sense to me was a wry anti-instruction guide. Much to my horror (and a little to my perverse amusement), I'd started noticing some of the more plaintive essays that I'd written about various missteps I'd made in my life being shared in autism parenting groups like they were useful templates for raising happy, healthy autistic kids. In one case, a story about how I'd used TV shows to help me figure out social skills in the absence of any better options was being passed around as something that might be worth a try—as if anyone should take those kind of cues from a nerd who writes about gaining insight into workplace dynamics from *NewsRadio* for the internet. If people felt any inclination to treat my major falls and minor lifts like a how-to manual, I figured I could at least try to warn them about how ill-advised and occasionally impossible that pursuit is.

So here you have my fifteen uneasy steps to an autistic "success" story. You're welcome to call this real. I hope you do. Just please don't try this at home.

STEP ONE

Be born to Jane and Dan Kurchak

I WAS BORN AT 8:36 A.M. ON FEBRUARY 7, 1982, IN NORTH YORK, Ontario. By 9:36 a.m., I'd received my first completely unsolicited opinion on the value of my existence.

This exchange was treated as an amusing side note when my parents told me the story of my birth as a child: One borderline blizzard-ridden night in Toronto, my mother's water broke after watching a bad movie.[2] My father and grandfather dug our car out of a snowdrift in a panic while my grandmother calmly assured everyone that labour is a long process, and they still had plenty of time to get to the hospital. When the car was finally free, they all piled in and hurtled toward North York General, where the kind nurses repeated my grandmother's assurances. But I beat the doctor to the delivery room, quietly taking in my new surroundings with wide eyes and a deep purple bruise sprawling across my tiny head.

By the time my father managed to put on scrubs, I was already cleaned up and hanging out in a bassinet. He walked over to it, and we made eye contact (the real miracle in all

....
2 Late in the editing process, Mom and Dad informed me that this long-alluded-to "bad movie" was, in fact, *Zardoz*. Which is a classic and easily my favourite film about red panties and evil penises. My whole life is a lie.

11

of this, given that we were both later diagnosed as autistic). Then he reached his hand toward me and I grabbed his baby finger.

Still in awe of this simple but profound moment of connection with the new human he'd just unleashed on the world, Dad went back to Mom's room and was greeted by the husband of the woman in the next bed.

"Hey! What did you have?" this alpha male type asked my gentle father.

"A girl," he beamed.

"Oh, too bad! *I* had a *boy*," he puffed.

My father was genuinely wounded; my mother, bemused. She had thought she was having a boy—and had assembled onesies and potential names accordingly—but had no actual preference in the matter. "Other mothers seemed to know what they were having, and I thought I should do that, too," she'd tell me. "I didn't want a boy; I just wanted to be right!"

Mom cast aside her dreams of psychic maternal instinct without regret, and my parents took me home to a childhood where people were accepted for who and what they were, girls could wear a lot of pre-purchased blue clothing and men who only cared about having boys became minor villains in a more important tale.

As a teenager, I tried to fashion this into a post–riot grrrl origin story about a girl who had been pitted against boys from her first breath and now lived to prove everyone wrong. I treated every accomplishment in my life as a knock against boyhood in general, and that man's precious son in particular. ("I'd like to see *you* place second in a mathlete competition, Boy Who Was Also Born At North York General On 02/07/82!")

In my twenties, I learned that I'd been born on my exact due date and wondered if the events of my birth had actually prophesied my life. In a last-minute flurry, not a moment too soon or too late, and with great damage to my head, is exactly how I meet all of my deadlines.

Now I tend to think that the meaning of my birth story—if there is one at all—lies in how well it establishes the parenting techniques that have kept me loved, alive and about as content as possible thus far. My parents brought me into this world with almost no expectations or preconceived notions of who or what I should be. They welcomed me as-is, and chucked whatever ideas no longer suited our reality. They loved the baby they had for who she was, not for the ways in which she lived up to their desires or might do so in the future. And if someone wasn't on board with that, they could go fuck themselves.

Because I am an autistic person who appears to have achieved some of the arbitrary hallmarks we attribute to successful adulthood—like living semi-independently, working, getting married and performing basic social tasks without melting down in public—I am often treated like someone who should have a clue as to how others might do those things. I am not. I'm not convinced that I've done anything to make it to this point in my life that should be emulated by another human being. If I have, it certainly wouldn't have been possible without the foundation my parents built for me. What good is my example for anyone else when it's inextricably linked with my good fortune?

I don't believe in fate. It's a ridiculous, solipsistic concept and it's arrogant and heartless for anyone to believe that any privilege they might have over others is *meant to be*. I do think that a number of things about our lives come down to the fluky circumstances of how we came to exist, though. You're born in a body that is either celebrated or brutalized by our society. You're born into means or you aren't. No matter what chances we might be granted after that, no matter what we do with them, there's still so much that comes down to that initial luck.

I was born with a neurology that is rarely compatible with the world we live in. I am overwhelmed by its scents, sounds and sights and can only contain that sensory overload with great effort. I have no natural instincts to help me navigate society, either socially or physically, and compensating for that takes even more effort. I was also born at a time when few knew how to recognize these symptoms in girls. And I grew up in a small town that offered very little in terms of resources for such a kid—or many other misfits who might be willing to like them. On a global scale, this is far from the worst lot. It has been regularly challenging, demoralizing and terrifying on a personal level, though.

I also happened to be born to two loving people who took all of the above in stride. They might not have known why I behaved the way I did, but they knew that I was different and, through trial and error, they worked to find solutions that helped me feel safe, secure and loved. With care and practicality, they assessed my challenges and addressed them on their own terms. My progress was never measured against other children, or against a hypothetical child they'd imagined having before they wound up with me. I never felt—I still never feel—like I was an embarrassment, a disappointment or a burden to them.

I'm not sure it ever even occurred to them to approach the situation any other way. In the days following my eventual diagnosis at age twenty-seven, I started to list some of my more obviously autistic behaviours as a child. "Seriously," I said with a laugh. "At no point did you stop and wonder if maybe something was wrong?"

"Not wrong." Mom shrugged. "If anything, we wondered if the other kids were weird."

Just because I was never made to feel like my childhood was wrong or bad doesn't mean that it was easy for any of us, though. My issues included:

· disrupted sleeping patterns that resulted in an inability to sleep through the night for the first three and a half years of my life, and a struggle to sleep through the night thereafter

· a sensitivity to loud noises that often manifested in terrified screaming episodes and/or silent shaking panic attacks whenever our seventies-era dishwasher was turned on

· a sensitivity to touch that made nail and hair cutting and tooth cleaning painful in a way I couldn't begin to articulate to anyone. This led to a number of screaming meltdowns at the dentist

· a sensitivity to scent strong enough that going near the laundry detergent aisle while shopping caused a level of discomfort in my chest that I didn't know how to explain, so I called it heartburn

· sensitivities to texture and taste that significantly limited my diet

· rapid, wordy and relatively monotone speech patterns that mostly annoyed other kids and unnerved adults

· extreme reactions to other people's emotions; I regularly tried to crawl under chairs and hide when my mom expressed displeasure at whatever the Oilers were doing during hockey games

· a toilet training learning curve that I am only comfortable describing as atypical

· massive difficulties when it came to socializing with my peers

- an awkward gait and low body awareness
- narrow, intense and occasionally age-inappropriate fields of interest, including dinosaurs, the *Titanic*, *Max Headroom* and David Lynch's *Dune*
- repetitive movement patterns like leg twitching and playing with my hair in very specific ways
- an imperfect grasp of boundaries; if I happened to be talking to someone on their way to the bathroom, I would follow them right into the bathroom and not realize I wasn't supposed to be there unless they explicitly asked me to leave[3]
- a strong aversion to change and little ability to handle it
- anxiety surrounding public outings, particularly going to restaurants

(I have chosen to list the above as simply and dryly as I can because I am tired—both as a writer and a human being—of trying to say it any other way. I don't know how to shoehorn all of these pieces of my past and present into a compelling narrative that manages to suitably convince other people of my autistic legitimacy while also affording me a modicum of privacy and dignity. And I don't think embellishing a bunch of symptoms that anyone can google with lurid personal anecdotes is really the best use of my time, energy or word count. I'm also hoping that anyone who came to this book hoping for a voyeuristic dose of autism tragedy and/or inspiration will get bored and leave now.)

I realize that my parents are not perfect. My love for them and my appreciation for what they've done for me do not come from an idealized fantasy, or an unwillingness to admit that they're fallible. They made mistakes, as all parents do,

....
3 If I followed you into a bathroom as a child, please know that I am very sorry and mortified. And still haunted by those moments when I still can't sleep.

regardless of what neurodevelopmental disorders their children may or may not have. There were plenty of things that went unnoticed due to a lack of awareness and resources, or simply no context for figuring out when something that seemed like a cute quirk might be a sign of a deeper issue. For example, I'm not sure my mom realized what "Tide gives me heartburn" actually meant until I sent her a draft of this essay. But the things my parents did notice and the way they handled them made all of the difference in the world to me.

They gently tested the limits of my sensory and physical concerns through trial and error. Did soaking my hands in the tub before clipping my nails make the experience less painful for me? It at least took the edge off. Would testing out different hair salons help me to find a place where trims might be more comfortable? Eventually. Could dishwashing be scheduled for times when I wouldn't be home? Often. Could they add variety to my diet by allowing me to try small bites of new things in the comfort of our own home? Not so much.

When my gait issues became pronounced enough that I sometimes tripped over my own toes, they told me that sometimes people need help with their feet and took me to an orthopedic clinic. When their treatments—which included slathering a bunch of gross foam on the side of my favourite pair of pink running shoes—failed to lead to any changes beyond making me miserable, they scraped the offensive foam off and told me that we'd figure something else out. We never did, but the issue gradually faded over time. I still have to be aware of it when I run, but it's no longer a major concern for me.

What couldn't be changed, or couldn't be changed without significant pain and trauma, was accepted. When it became clear that my eating issues weren't just average pickiness and that some foods seemed to inspire almost violent physical discomfort, they constructed a diet for me that would at least keep me alive and fairly healthy—if not perfectly in line with the Canada Food Guide. My movements and speaking habits weren't hurting anyone, as far as they were concerned, so Mom and Dad simply let them be and suggested that I could ignore the many people who told me that they made me seem weird, gross or flighty. They warned me about changes in our lives as far in advance as they could, and patiently allowed me to work through my responses to them without making me feel like I was disappointing them for being unable to go with the flow.

What they had no desire to change, they embraced. To them, my interests weren't obsessions that needed to be quashed for my well-being and potential social acceptance. They were signs of a mind that should be encouraged. They engaged my curiosity with books, videos, conversations and anything else that might be related to a particular topic. As a child, I spent a lot of time visiting historical societies for events on the *Titanic*. I even had the chance to see Dr. Robert Ballard speak and have him sign my copy of his book, *The Discovery of the Titanic*, when I was five. (He asked me if I wanted to go into his line of work when I grew up. I already knew I wanted to write, but I said yes, because I didn't want to offend the man who had discovered my favourite shipwreck. "Then make sure you work hard on your math!" he said. "We don't have mathematics in kindergarten," I replied, as five-year-olds do.)

Passions that had less obvious educational merit were also bolstered, because my parents saw value in me having things in my life that were for pure enjoyment, or an escape from a world that was starting to become a little hard for me. When I couldn't stop talking about Max Headroom[4] thanks

....

4 A creepy but compelling artificial intelligence character that began life as a subversive parody of superficial media talking heads and then inexplicably became the face of the ill-fated New Coke campaign.

to the infamous Coke campaign in 1986, they carefully compiled clips that were suitable for a child to watch and shared them with me. The following Christmas, they found a Max Headroom logo at a custom T-shirt booth and spent ages carefully cropping the image until it fit on the tiniest sweatshirt available. I still have it. I acquired a *Dune* colouring book in a similar spirit.

Other things could only be endured with ceaseless patience—or at least the illusion of ceaseless patience in front of a scared and overly sensitive child who sometimes couldn't do any better. We can joke fondly about it now, but my forty-two-consecutive-month campaign against a full night's sleep nearly broke my parents. They managed to hone hour-of-the-wolf parenting into a fine art by the end of this waking nightmare. They took shifts with me. Sometimes they'd take me down to the living room, set up camp in front of the TV and repeatedly play my favourite segments from *Singin' in the Rain* and the Winnie the Pooh movie. Or they'd sit me at the small table they'd put next to their bed and hand me some crayons so that I could blissfully colour while they watched over me in semi-consciousness. They were exhausted. Even in a cheery doodle that my father made me during one of our late-night adventures and later pasted in my baby book, you can see the weariness in my cartoon parents' faces. But my own memories of that time are happy ones. Their desire for me to sleep was always presented to me as concern for my own well-being, not as a way to be less of a pain to them.

Introducing me to public social outings, particularly restaurants, was another years-long process. When I was a baby, my parents had been able to take me almost anywhere, but I grew more anxious about eating in public, and being in loud rooms with strange lighting, as I got older. Once it became clear to them that this was an ongoing concern, my parents started telling me about our plans further in advance, so I had time to prepare myself. If it was feasible, they sometimes gave me the option of staying home instead—one I rarely took, because I loved the idea of going to restaurants and desperately did want to be able to enjoy them like everybody else I knew. When I got there and almost inevitably started feeling sick, they'd take turns whisking me off to the bathroom or to get some air outside.

As I got older, I started to feel guilty about how my sudden raging stomach problems were cutting into their social time, but they always made it clear that they didn't resent me for it. They must have wondered what the hell their lives had come to at some points. My mother spent one of her birthdays sitting in a bathroom stall at Toronto's late, lamented Organ Grinder,[5] listening to me dry heave to the tune of "Happy Birthday." My cousin had put in a request with the live organ player to celebrate the occasion, but I started feeling violently ill before he got to it. When the time came, Mom refused to leave my side. But she made it clear—as my parents always did—that she knew I couldn't help it and knew how hard I was trying. It took a lot of effort on all of our parts, and a lot of time—I think my restaurant-based anxiety outlived the Organ Grinder—but we were finally able to get to the point where outings like that were actually enjoyable for all of us.

Anything that might embarrass me, or make me a target for other kids' bullying and other adults' snap judgements, was kept more private. I have no recollection of my toilet training ever being brought up outside of our family unit. I remember thinking that I probably wasn't normal based on what I watched other kids go off to do on their own at

....

5 A musical restaurant franchise that specialized in loud decor, live organ performances and the kind of pizza we thought was really good in the eighties. In retrospect, the place was a sensory-overloading hell, but I have always valued kitsch and glorious nonsense over my well-being.

family functions and preschool, but my parents were quick to assure me that kids learned at different speeds. If they had any fears or frustrations, they either kept them to themselves, or quietly shared them with people who wouldn't—and didn't—use them against me at any point.

Dental visits, the cause and location of a large percentage of my public meltdowns, were somewhat mitigated by the aid and the saint-like patience of my dentist grandfather. I knew that how I was responding to procedures wasn't normal, either. I was actually deeply embarrassed by how much I cried and screamed through the simplest of treatments. But I didn't know how to stop myself, either. Everything hurt so much, I was so scared and having to worry about what a problem child I was becoming only left me less capable of managing my behaviour. So he started welcoming me into the office after hours, when it was quieter and felt safer to me. Softly and calmly, he would explain what needed to be done, and then work through the process, pausing to allow me to wail as needed, catch my breath and try again. Then he'd tape a two-dollar bill[6] to the side of his exam lamp and tell me that it was mine if I could make it through.

I don't want to give anyone the impression that I was spoiled, though. Enough people made that assumption when I was growing up—often outright scolding my parents for it in front of me—and I'm nervous that any description of their flexible parenting style will only perpetuate that idea. I was definitely sheltered, and possibly coddled. I was occasionally, as I've just confessed above, lightly bribed. But I never lived a life free of consequence, boundaries or guidance. My family worked hard to ensure that I would be polite, responsible and kind. If anything I was doing was physically

....
6   A Canadian banknote—and subject of one of my favourite *Kids in the Hall* visual gags—that was replaced with the toonie in 1996.

or emotionally hurtful to anyone, including myself, I was immediately stopped, and they made sure that I knew why I should never do that again. My intentional misbehaviour was punished appropriately. I simply wasn't made to suffer for things that they could tell weren't in my control.

Maybe I was a little indulged by how loving and encouraging—and how safe—the bubble of our small family was. I was oblivious about a number of things during my school years, but I knew that some of the other kids were openly envious of how nice my parents were. Interacting with my fellow autistic adults and listening to many of their stories has only made me feel more fortunate. I've worked hard to survive and piece together a life for myself since those early days. I still struggle on a daily basis. But I was given a head start on so many of my peers. My best-case-scenario childhood means that I can face all of those challenges without also having to grapple with the traumas and harmful coping mechanisms that can so easily manifest when those who love you the most are either unwilling or unable, for whatever reason, to raise the child they have, not the child they want or the child they feel they're supposed to have.

I know there are many great parents of autistic children out there. I'm friends with a few and in touch with many more who reached out after reading my articles. I've also talked to a couple of autistic adults who are as fond of their families and their efforts as I am of mine. Most of the stories people have shared with me, though, have been closer to horror than fairy tales. Parents who meant well but couldn't provide the support that their children were so desperately seeking. Parents who genuinely tried their best, but were misled by the prevailing attitudes of the time—or by the experts they trusted with their children's well-being. Exasperated and *tsk*ing relatives who couldn't understand why these kids couldn't just be normal. Abusers and their enablers.

So I struggle with how best to broach the topic of my near-idyllic parentage more than I struggle to address anything else. Which is saying a lot for someone with a prostrating, teeth-gnashing writing process and a disability that involves communication issues.

Mainly, I want to acknowledge how deeply I appreciate what they have done—and continue to do—for me, without rubbing my immense pleasure in the face of people who have suffered enough already.

It would be ignorant of me to make sweeping recommendations to my fellow autistic people or their parents when all I did to burst into this relatively great lot in life was show up in North York that one morning in 1982. It seems dickish to leave it at "Sorry you may not have been as lucky as I was!" though. Not to mention presumptuous to assume that my existence is so rarified that no part of it could be relatable or useful to someone else.

There are pieces of my history that, unfairly, aren't easy or possible for everyone to replicate. My parents are truly good and kind people, but their ability to apply those qualities to my needs didn't happen in a vacuum. Just as I lucked into my life with them, they were born into circumstances that allowed them to afford me this life.

We're white. Dad is second-generation Canadian. Mom's not even sure how far back her side became settlers here. We're all cisgender. They're straight. We were what I call middle class–adjacent. We never had much money—my father's employment was sporadic, which I now believe was a direct result of his own undiagnosed autism—but we had enough support from extended family to ensure that we would never go without food or shelter. My support needs as an autistic person were and are low (this doesn't mean that I'm just quirky or a little weird, or that I only experience "mild" symptoms; it simply means that I do not require significant assistance for my well-being and safety). My incredible clinginess as a child seems to have staved off any wandering impulses.

These things gave them the time to stay up with me every night, give me as much attention as they felt I required and to wait through however long it took me to process change and work through all of the things that needed to be done in a day. As harshly as they were judged for my behaviour, it was a fraction of what people of colour regularly face for similar parenting choices, and they never had to worry about how it would reflect on our race or ethnicity. I'm sure they were judged for our lack of money. I seem to recall at least one classmate's mother presuming that my issues were a manifestation of my general trashiness. But we were just comfortable enough that they never felt any pressure to produce a child who would follow in their footsteps work-wise or surpass them for whatever reason. Providing for my basic health and needs was always within their reach. The teachers and medical professionals of the Niagara Region, where I grew up, might not have been able to recognize autism in an ostensibly bright girl in the eighties and nineties, but few looked at a small-town white girl and assumed her weirdness was the result of behavioural issues and questionable parenting, either.[7]

The aspects of autistic existence that I feel comfortable stating with some degree of universality are mostly raging downers: It's not an easy life for any of us. All of the

....

7 Although an exhausting number of people did want to blame every imperfection on my being an only child. My parents are still shamed for it. As if "Hey! We don't like your kid and think you fucked her up. You should have more!" is in any way a rational argument.

advantages in the world can't entirely erase the challenges, pain and prejudice we face. We might be inching toward more understanding and acceptance for autistic people, but those baby steps, no matter how vital, probably won't lead to significant changes in the overall quality of autistic life in our lifetimes. The world will judge our parents harshly. The world will judge us harder. No matter how much any parent wants to fix that for their child, they can't. My parents have been pumping the aforementioned love, patience and support into me for almost forty years now, and they still get panicked texts in the middle of the night when I can no longer tune out the overbearing buzz of a distant light or my own self-loathing.

Depending on my mood, the one positive shred of advice I do feel qualified to give the parents who contact me can feel either hollow or saccharine. But my past tells me it's true, and the histories that so many other autistic people have trusted me with tell me it's neither obvious nor common enough to be a platitude.[8] So I offer this: You can't stop or fix everything for your child. You won't always make the choices that are right for them. But there's power in trying, and in the love that fuels those efforts. There's power in the act of being on their side.

Mom and Dad might not be able to help me change whatever it is that I'm texting about at ungodly hours. They might not have the right words to ease my fears and sadness. But they can offer me an outlet, a place to take my deepest, rawest, least articulated fears, knowing they will never be held or twisted against me. They couldn't stop some random asshole from dismissing me as a disappointment while I was still drawing my first breaths, but they could make it

....

8 I suspect that this disparity between my relative bubble and the outside world is also responsible for my incongruous blend of bleeding-heart earnestness and bristling sarcasm.

clear, in words and action, that they've never agreed. Having those two in my corner hasn't solved everything. There are days when it doesn't even take the edge off. But it's still been life-sustaining.

In a perfect world, no child would ever hear another person question their worth as a human. In a survivable world, though, the least we can give them is the reassurance that those people are the bad guys. And the knowledge that they're wrong.

STEP TWO

Harden your heart. And the pieces of your body that rub against the inside seams when you wear jeans

SARTORIALLY, AT LEAST, THE EIGHTIES AND NINETIES WEREN'T the worst time to be autistic.

Sure, the tag situation was often untenable. Almost every piece of clothing—even some underwear—had a rough piece of fabric with prickly edges lurking out of some seam, which made wearing an outfit feel like you had at least three Princess and the Pea situations going on all over your body at any given time. And the inside of the fleece employed in most late-eighties sweatshirts had a habit of going from fuzzy, warm and welcoming to a pebbled nightmare that felt like rubbing gravel and sandpaper against your skin within six washes. But most of the era's major fashion trends were friendly to people with social and sensory issues who wanted to give the impression of fitting in without strapping various bits of fibre-based torture to their bodies every day.

I sailed through the late eighties and early nineties in a series of oversized T-shirts, often tied at one side, which were inoffensive save for the aforementioned tag torture. In winters, I wore stirrup pants, which had relatively thin, gentle seams and no annoying cuffs that might rub against my ankles. In summer, I ran around in neon bike shorts, which were smooth and soothingly tight against my body— and made me feel like a Fly Girl.[9] I spent the turn of the millennium in oversized rave-influenced gear (sans accessories) and Modrobes, a stylized hospital scrub pant that took Canadian universities, rock festivals and my heart by storm around that time.

In the middle, though, there was grunge and its seemingly mandatory denim.

Left to my own devices, I would have gladly skipped the entire scene. I was about as fond of its aesthetics as I was of its sound. Nirvana, Pearl Jam and a mass of other bands that got lumped together as a genre because they shared a physical location (Seattle) and/or a headspace (angry/sad) resonated deeply with many of my peers. But all I heard were fuzzy, distorted feelings alternately whispered and screamed through fuzzier and more distorted guitars. My earlier flirtations with jeans-wearing had been dreadful affairs that made me feel like I'd trapped my lower half in an iron maiden. The only clothing I hated more was corduroy pants, which felt like I'd trapped my lower body in an only slightly less rigid iron maiden that rattled my bones and eardrums every time my toed-in legs brushed the fabric against itself.

But my new school was thoroughly entrenched in some rich small-town Canadian facsimile of the subculture by the time I arrived as a scared transfer student in the fall of 1993. I couldn't afford any fancy things like individuality or an ounce of physical comfort if I was going to survive. So I began building my armour out of affected apathy, irony and distressed denim.

....

9 The Fly Girls were a dance troupe featured on *In Living Color*, a skit show that aired on Fox from 1990 to 1994 and had a massive influence on my developing fashion sense and awareness of racial inequality.

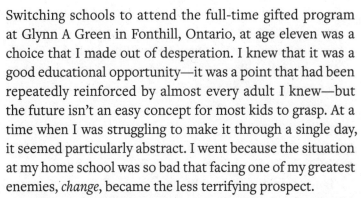

Switching schools to attend the full-time gifted program at Glynn A Green in Fonthill, Ontario, at age eleven was a choice that I made out of desperation. I knew that it was a good educational opportunity—it was a point that had been repeatedly reinforced by almost every adult I knew—but the future isn't an easy concept for most kids to grasp. At a time when I was struggling to make it through a single day, it seemed particularly abstract. I went because the situation at my home school was so bad that facing one of my greatest enemies, *change*, became the less terrifying prospect.

I was always different, always a little out of step with the other kids I came into contact with in my earliest years, but I didn't realize that was a problem until I started school. Preschool through grade three saw my gradual descent from awkward but tolerable to weird and loathsome. I did manage to make and keep one truly good friend during those years, but she went to another school. By grade four, the proper bullying had kicked in, although it took me a while to catch on.

Somewhere between grade three and grade five—I'm still not any clearer on the timeline—the group of girls I'd been hanging out with for the bulk of my school years decided that they no longer liked me. They failed to let me in on this conclusion, however. It's possible they tried to give me hints to move on, but if they did, I was incapable of reading them. (Whatever it is that allows the average person to pick up on subtle signs that what they're doing, saying or being isn't wanted was not among my alleged gifts and talents.) Whatever the case, they then pretended they were still my friends, because it made me an even easier target. They mined our conversations for things that could embarrass me, and scouted my home for things to steal when they visited.

When I finally called them on it, they moved on to full-blown psychological warfare. Favourite strategies included prank calls, writing on my clothes, stage whispering insults behind my back during class and following me around the playground, mimicking every single move I made during recess.

My general unlikeable aura left none of my other classmates particularly interested in coming to my defence, or any more welcoming of my attempts to hang out with them instead. So I woke up every school day feeling like my stomach was wrapped in swiftly tightening barbwire, tried to choke down some breakfast, sometimes coughed it right back up again and did my best not to give anyone the satisfaction of seeing me cry. Again. Then I aced some arbitrary tests that deemed me "talented" enough to go to a different school for a special program.

I resisted the opportunity at first because I didn't want to go somewhere new and meet new people. I didn't want to have to face my morning panic even earlier so that I could take the bus to this place. I didn't want to be somewhere far enough from my home in Welland that I couldn't go there for the brief respite lunch hour gave me. A part of me was afraid that the same thing would happen no matter where I went and that I'd face all of this extra aggravation for nothing. As far as I was concerned, homeschooling was the only truly safe option, but my parents didn't feel they were capable of providing it. Within another miserable year, though, I was willing to do anything to escape. A chance to start all over again and probably fail all over again was still better than no chance at all, so I took it.

Although I was far from optimistic about the potential of this new beginning, I swore to myself that I would do everything in my power to protect myself from being hated and targeted again. The only problem was, I didn't have a clue how to do that, or where to start. When you're not on the same social wavelength as anyone in your general vicinity, figuring out when people stop liking you isn't the only challenge. You also don't know *why* they don't like you.

So I made the kind of decisions that make sense to a scared and rudderless eleven-year-old desperate to become less of a target: I obsessively studied people and characters who weren't social pariahs and tried to reproduce anything that might play a part in the way other people responded to them. Then I hypercritically overanalyzed every interaction I had for any hints that I might be screwing up again.

It was under these circumstances that I came to believe that jeans were a life or death matter.

A couple of months into my time at GAG, I found myself in a casual conversation about clothing. In the middle of it, a girl who had, as far as I could tell, been nothing but nice to me said, "Sarah always wears sweatpants." It was, as far as I could tell, a completely neutral observation, a passing comment that wasn't even the focus of what she was actually saying. There was nothing in her tone or phrasing that I'd taught myself to recognize as judgemental, scolding, snide, mocking, passive aggressive or even gently discouraging. But I still panicked and overthought the situation, just to be safe.

I spent the rest of the day studying the kids in my class. I watched the other students file out after last period and looked at their lower halves in the hallway. At least 95 percent of them were in jeans. I looked down at my knit stirrup pants and felt embarrassed. I'd been so excited when I'd invested a chunk of my meagre back-to-school budget on them, so sure that they'd make me seem acceptable—or at least keep me off of a new bully's radar.

I was humiliated by my clothes, but I was even more ashamed by the naivety with which I'd chosen them. I'd learned absolutely nothing from my past mistakes, and I was about to get another extended emotional beating that

I deserved. My only hope was to buy jeans, somehow teach myself how to wear them without squirming and hope that I'd be forgiven for whatever it was that my "sweatpants" seemed to signal. And be even more careful next time.

I settled on a pair of light blue boot-cut jeans from Gap Kids for a number of reasons. I'd seen the brand on others and hoped that it might help obscure the fact that I wasn't nearly as well off as the upper-middle-class families who populated my new school's area code. The cuffs were just loose enough to keep them from constantly rubbing against my ankles and the waistband was fitting but not constricting. I also appreciated the sand wash, which made them a little more forgiving than the pairs I'd suffered in the past—they felt smooth when I rubbed my hands against my thighs.

The most inoffensive jeans that I had ever encountered were still jeans, though. While the treatments this denim had gone through made it more tolerable, the wrong side of the fabric wasn't as distressed and maintained the sandpapery texture I'd always hated encasing myself in. This abrasiveness was further compounded when multiple pieces of it came together and were bound with ropey thread on the inner thighs. Those seams still congealed into an even thicker, bulkier and more abrasive chunk right where I wanted it the least.

I've lived in relative harmony with jeans for over a quarter of a century now and I still don't understand how a pant style that invariably presses a massive chunk of hard fabric against one of the most sensitive areas of your body has enjoyed such enduring popularity. I'm even more baffled that we've seen no real evolution in this feature in the course of my lifetime. Or in the course of jeans' lifetime, for that matter. I still think I'd be a little more comfortable in a pair that provided some alternative.

Back then, though, the infamous crotch nub wasn't just a curiosity or mild annoyance, it was painful. My whole body tensed a little when I so much as anticipated making contact with it. The most delicate of brushes could sting. I briefly flirted with adding various bits of small padding to the area, but nothing dulled the sensation. All I could do was put them on, endure and try to conceal that I was walking around in a passably stylish torture chamber that scraped my skin and sent stabbing pains coursing through my pubic area.

The stealth suffering part came easily enough. I had developed a knack for hiding any outward signs of distress during my bullied phase, and those skills translated well to this new task. As for the rest, I just kept wearing the damned things and hoping that I'd eventually develop some callouses, or desensitize myself—or maybe just learn to live with the pain. For almost a year, I thought I'd have to settle for the latter but then, without me being really conscious of it happening, all of my problems with the pants started to fade. I lived in the same make and model until the advent of Modrobes. And I remain a semi-regular jeans person to this day. (Although I am writing this while enjoying another merciful trend: jeggings.)

I restructured most of my outer life—and did my best to adjust pieces of my inner one—through variations of this process: Observe. Mimic. Overanalyze. Catastrophize. Observe some more. Try again. Resort to self-flagellation and self-torture as necessary. Repeat. My areas of focus included my tone of voice, body language, wardrobe and appearance, and the music, stories and hobbies that I'd admit to liking in front of other people. Some attempts were painful. Some frustrating. Some still leave a bitter taste, while others have become amusing anecdotes. A few became second nature to me after my initial attack, but most require constant effort to maintain. I can't think of a single one that I'd recommend to a child in a similar position today.

I often invoke The Great Jeans Project of 1993 in discussions about autism services and interventions now. If you're not autistic, this might strike you as a random choice. A quirky example of a differently wired brain's unconventional thought process, if you're being generous. A spoiled "high-functioning" person's attempt to derail a conversation about the serious needs of children with real autism, if you're not. What could current industry standard techniques designed to reduce challenging behaviours and help autistic children reach their full potential have in common with the panicked and flailing self-improvement plans of a socially maladjusted child in the late twentieth century?

Quite a lot, actually.

Today's autistic kids have access to more informed medical and psychological professionals and a greater array of services than my cohort did—the bar was *low*—but the ideology behind much of what is available to them is still based on the same unchallenged assumptions: If an autistic kid does something differently, it's probably disordered. If they're struggling in any aspect of their lives, it's probably because of those disordered behaviours. If you fix the behaviour, you can improve the outcome.

I'm not exaggerating for dramatic effect, though I wish I were. Here's an example of Applied Behaviour Analysis, "considered by many researchers and clinicians to be the most effective evidence-based therapeutic approach demonstrated thus far for children with autism," taken from Autism Canada's overview of the treatment, written by Lara Pullen, Ph.D:[10]

....

10   Autism Canada, "ABA." See https://autismcanada.org/living-with-autism/
treatments/non-medical/behavioural/aba/.

By keeping a chart of the times and events both before and after Michael's tantrums, a parent might discover that Michael always throws a tantrum right after the lights go on at night without warning. Looking deeper at the behaviour, Michael's mother might also notice that her most natural response is to cuddle Michael in order to get him to calm down. In effect, even though she is doing something completely natural, the cuddling is reinforcing Michael's tantrum. According to the ABA approach, both the trigger (lights going on at night without a warning) and the reinforcer (cuddling) must be stopped. Then a more appropriate set of behaviours (like leaving the room or dimming the lights) can be taught to Michael, each one being reinforced or prompted as needed. Eventually, the hope is that this kind of approach will lead to a time when the lights can go on without warning and Michael will not throw a tantrum.

A superficial reading of my jeans story wouldn't look out of place next to the Michael scenario: I saw a potential problem, worked hard to modify my behaviour and saw some baseline results.

The three years I spent at Glynn A Green were the best years I spent in a physical school. (The bar was *low*.) I had a modest number of good experiences. I made a few genuine friends, including the sweatpants observer, who was later upset to find out that her comment had caused any concern. Empowered by the tiniest bit of self-esteem and a raging case of post-pubescent contrarianism, I somehow managed to take a few tiny steps toward trying to be myself again along the way. I was still disliked by many, still taunted and yelled at. I still spent every day dragging myself through the door with an elevated pulse and a churning stomach. But it was a measurable improvement nonetheless.

There are three addenda to the story that I want people to consider, though:

1. Once I settled into the jeans, shoes became an issue. The rich kids wore Doc Martens and made it perfectly clear that the rest of us were worse than the dirt on the bottom of their working-class factory boots appropriated as monied status symbols if we couldn't as well. They scrutinized any Doc-like footwear to determine whether it bore the brand's iconic yellow stitching or not. Anyone caught with imitation Docs was subject to intense mockery on the playground.

While visiting family over Christmas, my parents and I stumbled across a pair of kid's Docs on sale that fit my small feet and our tinier budget. They didn't look exactly like the full-grown version, but they were still Docs. Knowing how much I loved the style and the prospect of being hated less, Mom and Dad spent what little they had on a pair.

I proudly wore them to school on my first day back and was almost immediately confronted by two rich girls from yellow stitch quality control.

"Why are you telling people you have Docs?" one barked. "Those don't *look* like Docs."

I tried to explain myself and my shoes, but they were unconvinced. So I ripped the right one off my foot and handed it to them. After a thorough inspection of the stitches—and the soles, insoles and tags—they passed my bona fide Doc back to me with begrudging acceptance.

Sometimes I think about the sneers they wore throughout the exchange, the "we all know you don't really belong and we know you know it" so obvious in their every move that even I, who couldn't read shit, recognized it. Sometimes I think about how I stood there and took it.

2. After receiving a copy of our class photo from that year and studying it even more intensely than a nouveau riche queen bee with a poor weirdo's shoe and social prospects in her hands, I noticed that every single one of us was wearing jeans. One united, undifferentiated mass of oversized shirts on top of denim. My first feeling was relief. Finally, I'd gotten one thing right. But I also felt a pang of sadness.

3. Then I went to high school and had a year that made my GAG experience seem idyllic in retrospect. Instead of being miserable and bullied because I was so obviously different, I was miserable, borderline bullied for being a little off and falling into increasing despair that I could ever make things any better.

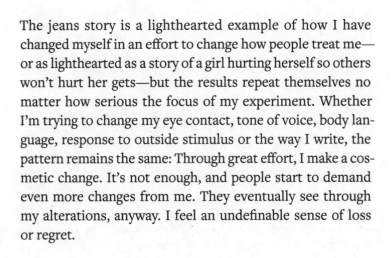

The jeans story is a lighthearted example of how I have changed myself in an effort to change how people treat me—or as lighthearted as a story of a girl hurting herself so others won't hurt her gets—but the results repeat themselves no matter how serious the focus of my experiment. Whether I'm trying to change my eye contact, tone of voice, body language, response to outside stimulus or the way I write, the pattern remains the same: Through great effort, I make a cosmetic change. It's not enough, and people start to demand even more changes from me. They eventually see through my alterations, anyway. I feel an undefinable sense of loss or regret.

The results aren't sustainable. Which is why I worry about any treatment that seems more invested in altering the outward signs of autism than helping a person cope with their causes.[11] Like poor hypothetical Michael and his reaction to turning the lights off. Did anyone try to figure out why the dark upset him so much? Did the ABA alleviate his fear, or merely disguise it? Does the treatment genuinely make his life a little easier, or does it make him easier for other people?[12]

I taught myself how to look more "normal," but I didn't learn how to preserve a sense of self-worth—or a sense of self—when I didn't look normal enough for others. I developed haphazard adaptation skills when what I really could have used was someone who could help me develop the skills and coping mechanisms I needed to navigate a world so confusing to me that I thought *pants* could solve anything.

....

11 Here's a practical example of what I mean by helping an autistic person develop coping mechanisms instead of superficially altering their behaviour: I was recently discussing nutrition with an occupational therapist who specializes in autistic children and teens. Most of them only eat a few foods, and she's been working on ways to make sure they get essential nutrients. Instead of putting these kids through treatments that would force them to eat the food, she has suggested vitamins. She usually recommends the chewable variety, because she's also noticed that many of her autistic clients have trouble swallowing pills. (This, by the way, is also how I work around my dietary and swallowing issues.)

12 If you're interested in learning more about the possible inefficacy and harm of ABA, I recommend reading "Lived Experiences of Applied Behaviour Analysis: Adult Autistic Reflections of Childhood Intervention" (https://pureportal.strath. ac.uk/en/publications/lived-experiences-of-applied-behaviour-analysis-adult-autistic-re) and "Early Intensive Behavioral Intervention (EIBI) for Increasing Functional Behaviors and Skills in Young Children with Autism Spectrum Disorders (ASD)" (https://www.cochrane.org/CD009260/BEHAV_early-intensive-behavioral-intervention-eibi-increasing-functional-behaviors-and-skills-young).

STEP THREE

Lie and/or obfuscate

FIVE MONTHS INTO MY ATTEMPT TO START A NEW, BULLY-ing-free life at a new school, I turned twelve. My efforts by then had not been a complete failure, so I decided to take a bold step toward being borderline normal: a birthday party.

My eleventh birthday party was a woeful affair that wouldn't have been out of place in an early Todd Solondz film.[13] I was still under the illusion that my bullies were my friends at that point, so I invited them. Whether their parents forced them out of some misguided sense of kindness/pity, or the girls themselves simply couldn't resist such a perfect setup, they came. The theme of the evening's proceedings was Friendships That Do Not Involve Birthday Girl Sarah Kurchak. The two ringleaders made crafts in celebration of their BFF-hood and delivered paeans to it during dinner and cake time. The others sat around awkwardly while I quietly stewed in a mix of jealousy and self-reproach for said jealousy. When I snuck off to cry in my room, I noticed that one of my video games wasn't where I'd left it. When I finally figured out that those girls hated me, I stopped blaming myself for misplacing it.

....
13 In other words, it was unseemly, awkward and potentially cringe-inducing.

A year later, I was in a better place. Sure, I remained raw and skittish from that experience, and so many others that happened in its wake, but I could go whole days without crying! I could wear jeans just like real people! And I was 20 to 45 percent sure that I had made a few friends who wouldn't abscond with my stuff and the remainder of my self-esteem if I invited them into my home. My desperate desire to be the kind of person who could have a birthday party slightly outweighed my lingering fear that something like that would happen again.

The risk was worth it. My twelfth birthday was filled with things you'd find in your average trifle of a family film about days gone by: people who liked each other, giggling, bonding, a bare minimum of passive aggression and an absence of stealth crying jags. There was also a discussion about boys that ranged from why they smelled so much to who we liked.

When it was my turn, my reticence came creeping back. This was exactly the kind of moment I'd been longing for when I wandered alone each recess at my old school, watching groups of girls huddle together and whisper their secrets to each other. There was a boy I liked—a smart, arty classmate of ours with floppy blond hair I'll call G—and I wanted nothing more than to share this with friends, to indulge in the giddy highs and lows of these new feelings with girls just as scared and confused and excited as I was. By that point, though, I was already painfully aware that I was not the kind of girl who boys liked, which made me question whether I could be the kind of girl who could tell other girls about boys at all.

I ran all of the potential social suicides through my head the way autistic savants calculate math problems in TV shows. The best-case scenario was that I would tell them I liked G, someone would tell G I liked him, he'd be grossed out and I'd be humiliated in front of my crush and comforted by my friends. Worst case? I would tell them I liked G, someone would tell G I liked him, he'd be grossed out and I'd be humiliated in front of my crush and mocked by my maybe not friends. Not liking my odds, I came up with another brilliant solution: I told them that I liked the same boy they did. A dull, smug rich boy named D who looked like Butt-Head[14] made flesh.

Unfortunately, my risk aversion was also worth it. My big secret came out about a week later, carelessly but not maliciously spilled in a series of ungainly moments in art class when Sweatpants Observer and I were assigned to share a table and a tub of papier-mâché paste with G and D.

A friend and party attendee at an adjacent table said that she hoped things didn't get weird. Sweatpants started giggling nervously. One of them, I don't remember who, eventually squealed, "He knooooows." Which D then confirmed by shrugging and mumbling, "Lots of girls like me."

His slimy smugness made me want to give up the ruse and point out that I didn't, and G was googolplex times cuter than he would ever be. But I couldn't tell if G's laugh was mocking or sympathetic, and I didn't dare think it was envious, so I looked down at my project and pretended to be oh my god, so embarrassed by this totally real revelation. Mercifully, empty-eyed resignation to the harsh realities of life can pass for doe-eyed romantic humiliation when everyone is busy applying sticky, grainy pieces of newspaper to a balloon with two toilet paper rolls taped to it. I spent the rest of the period toiling way at my pile of garbage that I would later try to convince my teacher was a statue of Nancy Kerrigan[15] and reconciling myself to some big truths. People

....

14   One half of the giggling sophomoric nineties cartoon duo Beavis and Butt-Head. Great to laugh at on TV, nothing to lust over in corporeal form.

15   It was the winter of 1994 and we were all obsessed with the attack on Olympic figure skater Kerrigan orchestrated by her rival Tonya Harding's ex-husband. I wasn't a fan of either skater, but I did have a perverse soft spot for Harding because I was also an uncouth poor kid trying to survive in rich people territory. Which I expressed through terrible art.

don't have to hate you to hurt you. Your secrets probably aren't safe with anyone. Whatever. We're all alone until we die. Which we also do alone.

This is how I learned to keep worrying and love the lie.

The autistic struggle with lying, both as a concept and an activity, is fairly well documented as far as issues that actually affect autistic people go. It's appeared everywhere from a special episode of *The Good Doctor* to autistic parenting memes that float around Pinterest and Facebook. Some autistic people proudly celebrate our bluntness and directness. Even autism parents usually prone to more tragedy-based narratives have embraced the inability to lie as one of the few silver linings of raising kids on the spectrum. Some experts worry that our inability to detect lies makes us vulnerable to abuse[16] while others see it as yet another deficiency on our parts. (In a blog post called "Lying in Autism: A Cognitive Milestone" for the Autism Research Institute, Stephen M. Edelson, Ph.D., chalks up our struggles with lying to a theory of mind issue.[17] Apparently we can't understand that other people have other thoughts, feelings and perspectives. And we assume that everyone can read our minds. And it's a great victory if we overcome these failings and ... lie to your face.)

While I'm glad that people seem to know it's a thing for us, I don't think any of the above takes are fair or accurate. We are not more evolved life forms who have moved beyond

16 University of Kent, "People with ASD Risk Being Manipulated Because They Can't Tell When They're Being Lied To," *ScienceDaily*. See www.sciencedaily. com/releases/2018/05/180522114817.htm.
17 Stephen M. Edelson, "Lying in Autism: A Cognitive Milestone." *Autism Research Institute*. See www.autism-help.org/points-lying-milestone-autism.htm.

simple human conventions. Nor are we "special" kids who are too pure for the complexities of normal human interaction. And I'm pretty sure we're not blank little monsters who don't realize that you're people, too.

As far as I can figure, we're just not wired for lies. It's a behaviour that exists as part of a social structure crafted by and for non-autistic people. It is, in fact, a behaviour designed to convince people who exist within that social structure, who know the rules and can play by them, to believe in things that are not true. The tells that non-autistic people focus on to help them separate honesty from lies are things we struggle with, like body language and eye contact. Of course we're going to suck at the whole thing! Lying is completely counterintuitive to those of us who have literal thinking styles, a fondness for well-articulated rules and a strict moral code. We have no innate aptitude for telling lies or detecting them, and navigating the seemingly arbitrary lines that normal people draw between good ones and bad ones can feel a bit Kafkaesque. Many of us can learn your ways, though. Some of us have no choice if we want to survive.

Like many women, I have given a man a fake phone number. I wanted to be honest and tell him that I wasn't interested. Life, love and lust would be so much easier if we were able to be frank about our feelings and intentions. A nagging part of me considered just giving it to him, anyway, because constantly having your opinions, perspectives and behaviour questioned has a pesky habit of undermining your autonomy like that. But a lifetime of studying other people— and taking self-defence lessons and paying basic attention to the news—has taught me that strange men don't always respond well to open rejection. So I weighed my options and lied to protect myself. Like many autistic people, I apply the same risk aversion to sharing the details of my life that I do with my digits.

I am inclined to tell the truth. I'm also inclined to offer more than was probably asked. I veer toward guileless disclosure and borderline oversharing when left to my own devices. Saying anything other than exactly what I meant took some getting used to. And the idea of white lies blew my mind as a child. One day all of the trusted adults in my life were telling me that honesty is the best policy. The next, Mom was taking me aside to explain that, when you're a guest at someone's home, you don't have to tell them that their carrots taste like dental office air[18] when they ask how you liked your dinner. My brain craves things that follow rules and things that make sense and this whole fibbing to protect other people seemed to do neither. After years of being told that lying was wrong, I was suddenly being told that it's actually good sometimes? And I was supposed to just magically guess when that works and when it doesn't? I love moral ambiguity in art, but I'd prefer if life were at least a bit easier to navigate.

"I totally have a crush on D" was the first lie I consciously decided to tell to deceive someone else for my own ends—and it was the first time I understood the power of doing so. I wasn't perfect before then. I'd told a few dramatically exaggerated whoppers for whatever reason all kids feel possessed to pull that shit. I'd flirted with evasion and sometimes been less than forthcoming when I had a feeling that I was about to get in trouble for something. I sometimes failed to understand the normal boundaries of pretend and fantasy in ways that were unintentionally untruthful. But looking at a situation, thinking through the possible outcomes, choosing to go with a deception that would benefit me and following through on it was new to me.

What I initially took away from this experience was that lying, no matter how little sense it made, was an

---

18 For the record, carrots *do* taste like a dentist office smells, though.

absolute necessity because you can't trust anyone and friendship/trust/solidarity/love/any modicum of comfort in this world were also lies. I was freshly twelve, careening toward puberty, nursing a very real case of unrequited like and fostering a fake one as some sort of Band-Aid for this life-ruining devastation. And I had just discovered The Cure.[19] What other conclusion could anyone come to under those circumstances? With time, new awkward crushes, self-reflection and a greater understanding of the full spectrum of emotions represented in The Cure's oeuvre, I was able to appreciate this as a more nuanced learning experience.

I still aim to be as open and direct as possible. It's a personal preference as much as an ideological stance. My life is better when I can be myself and genuinely know where I stand with other people. But I also understand that the world we live in does not always make that possible. In a society that doesn't allow everyone to comfortably—or even safely—be true to themselves and each other, lying can keep us alive. As long as lies are used as a tool of deception, abuse or even simple carelessness or selfishness, we'll also need to wield them as a defence against those things.

I can and will lie to protect other people and to take care of myself. If someone who is vulnerable in some way comes to me in confidence, like a closeted autistic person looking for advice—which has happened a lot since I gained a modicum of attention for my writing on autism—I will do what is necessary to protect their secrets. I'll guard my own the same way. Fibs are useful when I want to manage my issues in daily life without overexposing myself or worrying that I'm making anyone else uncomfortable. "I'm grounded"

....
19   Formed in 1978, The Cure are an iconic British goth band whose music tackles sadness, loss, cats, the heartbreaking limits of interpersonal connection, fluctuations in affection over the course of a basic work week and the entirety of the human experience.

came in handy when I'd get invited to a rare party as a teenager, almost immediately become too panicked about this exciting new social opportunity to be able to leave the house, and then need a way to decline that might not dissuade the inviter from trying again in the future. If I need to cancel plans for autism-related reasons, I'll say that I'm not feeling well. If someone follows that up with an "Oh no, what's wrong?" I'll default to a simple physical issue like saying my stomach or head hurts instead of saying that I'm on the verge of a meltdown because I mismanaged my schedule again and the thought of using public transit has made me forget how to regulate my breathing.

I don't think I'm good at outright lies and fact fudging, though. I can hear the cartoonish catch in my voice every time I spout one. But if autism has robbed me of whatever innate aptitude normal people have for this stuff, it has at least left me with inscrutable facial expressions and body language. They might make people question me when I am telling the truth on occasion, but they also leave people unable to know for sure when I'm not. I figure it's only fair because I have made no improvements in the field of being able to read anything the rest of you do. I default to wide-ranging suspicion when I'm feeling cynical and wide-eyed embrace of everything at face value when I'm not. Or I can study patterns of behaviour and make decent predictions based on that data. But making a sound judgement in real time? I'm as fucked as I ever was.

The delivery and reception of a mild truth blurring is actually far more comfortable territory for me. The gentler acts of not saying what you mean or meaning what you say—whether they be in the form of figurative language, irony, sarcasm or evasion—all threw me as child. With careful study and imitation, though, I've come around to most of them.

I find a lot of figurative language a silly non-autistic affectation, but the others can be quite useful. Irony came with a steep learning curve, but coming of age in the nineties gave me almost limitless opportunities to practice. My sarcasm process was a lot like a hero's journey in a martial arts flick: I was humiliatingly bad at it, the complete opposite of a natural, so I hid away and spent years studying under crotchety experts (I watched a lot of *Blackadder*[20]). Eventually, through hard work and determination, I was able to become a master in my own right. Together, irony and sarcasm formed the best exoskeleton an overly tender-hearted bullied kid could ask for. If you feel too exposed, you can retreat behind a shrug. Do or love something that isn't acceptable? Well, maybe you didn't *really* mean it.

Those two might be my favourite tools of misdirection—I consider them some of non-autistic culture's finest contributions—but evasion is my most useful one. Along with its buddies obfuscation and lies of omission, evasion became my sentinel long before I knew what it was.

This relationship began in my childhood, when my parents were first confronted with evidence that their kid might not be quite like the others. With each new idiosyncrasy, they were faced with a choice: Who do we tell, and how do we tell them? Do we treat this as a problem that we can complain about in the company of others? An embarrassing folly the whole family can tease her about in "good nature" for the rest of her days? Something they could try to explain to a disapproving stranger to possibly gain a touch of sympathy?

Each time, they chose the course of action that shielded my vulnerabilities from the world. Whatever might be

---

20 A dry and biting historical comedy that originally aired on the BBC between 1983 and 1989. I was introduced to the show when it aired in reruns on TVO in the early nineties and subsequently raided my local video rental store for their neglected VHS copies of the series.

"wrong" with me was kept between us. Or between us and my medical professionals, if necessary. If they ever needed to go to someone else to complain, blow off some steam or share their fears, it must have been someone equally careful, because none of it ever came back to me. If there was any risk that I'd be misunderstood, preyed upon or further ostracized, they'd come up with alternate explanations for curious or nosy onlookers.

"Sarah's not feeling well" could mean "Sarah is hiding in another room and sobbing because she thinks she's ruined another family event and she doesn't know how or why," "Sarah is having another anxious episode in a restaurant restroom and she doesn't know why and she feels defeated and humiliated" or even "Sarah has been waking up literally shaking with fear every day this week, and we're hoping another fake sick day home from school might give her a chance to breathe."

"Sarah likes the *Titanic*" was a great euphemism for "Sarah has been talking about nothing but a nautical disaster for a week straight, our whole lives revolve around this boat, but at least it keeps her from bringing up Chernobyl again."

If we were walking with other people, something like "I think now is a good time to cross the street" could be employed to safely whisk me away from any chipped paint jobs or garish transoms in our path without getting into any "our child is terrified by certain textures and architectural features. We don't know why, but we see no need to push the issue."

Potentially taboo subject matter like toilet training snafus, dietary concerns, atypical behaviours and attachment anxiety could be glossed over in conversations with others. Any questions that might touch upon sensitive territory could be deflected if need be. My parents never tried to suggest that I was perfect when they were dealing with other adults. They were just careful to make sure that discussing my problems would not result in further problems for me. Even if they were unfairly criticized by other people who couldn't see the whole picture—chided for coddling or spoiling me when they were only addressing my needs the best way they knew how—they wouldn't spill any secrets that might take the heat off of them.

When I was old enough to start making my own decisions about how I wanted to present myself to the world, I was able to make those choices with a relatively clean slate. Sure, people knew I was a weird little girl and many preferred to keep their distance, but they didn't know the depth of it, or the possible roots of it. Being known as a kid who, say, pooped and hit herself comes with a stigma that's hard to live down as you grow up. Being strange for undefined reasons at least gives you a fighting chance.

I took it. What I couldn't beat out of myself and what I couldn't fake, I concealed by whatever means necessary. If sights, sounds or smells were bothering me, I'd try to deflect attention before anyone could notice. I started cultivating non-committal answers for all sorts of questions that might pry too deeply into an inner self I didn't trust anyone to accept. I learned to have whole conversations in which I revealed little to nothing about myself at all. I developed some skill in the fine millennial art of framing serious shit as self-deprecating jokes. (Like most broken creative types, I am the owner of a Twitter account littered with ostensibly playful quips about my anxiety, depression, dissociation episodes and executive dysfunction.)

Perhaps a normal person would simply call this setting boundaries. But I am not a normal person. In addition to being autistic, I am also a writer. As the latter, I suspect that I have an entirely different idea of what can and should be revealed than the average person. It's one of the many questionable personality traits that coalesce to convince people like me that taking up such a wretched calling is a good idea.

As an autistic, I've just never felt like I'm allowed much in the way of privacy. The more different you appear from other people, the more those people need to know why you're not like them. And they can be very forceful about it. I know so many visibly disabled people who are regularly approached by strangers demanding to know "what happened" to them. Many are blatantly rude when they don't receive a detailed answer. When people ask me why I move certain ways or do certain things—or why I'm so bloody awkward—I feel neither comfortable nor justified in plainly telling them to back off. When I tell someone that I'm autistic and they launch into a series of questions about my symptoms, my functions and why I'm not exactly like this other autistic person they met one time, I feel like I owe everyone a comprehensive follow-through. Like I need to prove myself to my interrogator and spread greater awareness for the community.

Writing about my autism has only exacerbated these problems. My impulse to (over)share and my need to protect myself are now in a constant battle, and my sense of obligation to the community is egging them both on from the sidelines. What can and should I say to satisfactorily establish my autism cred and provide enough background for an uninitiated audience while still affording myself a modicum of privacy? What do I owe, if anything, to readers who approach me, challenging me for information about my background? How do I argue for better representation and greater awareness while still maintaining the illusions and elusions that have helped me make it this far? That I might still require to keep going?

So-called "high-functioning" autism, at least as I experience it, is mostly smoke and mirrors. Yes, I might have certain advantages in our society that some of my fellow autistics might not have. I can speak and my cognitive processing speed allows me to take in information, break it down and respond to it at a rate that often helps me to keep up conversations and appearances with non-autistic people. But not looking obviously autistic to the untrained eye is not the same thing as not really being autistic. The lies and the evasions that I learned as a child aren't just coping mechanisms that I had to employ to earn my tiny place in society. They're also things I need to maintain to stay there.

Someone can see me semi-successfully engaging at a party and have no idea that I've spent a percentage of that night hiding in various quiet corners and nervously texting a loved one (usually Mom) for pep talks—or that I'll require days to recover from it. You might see me out shopping and have no idea that I've spent untold hours researching a map of the mall to locate all of the bathrooms, and that I've ducked into half of them to have a good cry or shake when the sounds, smells and general emotions of so many other people packed into a shiny capitalist hellhole get to be too much for me. And if you ask me how I manage the above, I will probably pick and choose which details I will actually share with you with great care and excessive anxiety. I am not ashamed to be autistic. I'm not embarrassed by my needs or issues. But I am hyper-aware of how other people react to them, and I'm not the bravest when it comes to risking scorn and rejection.

I don't outright lie or misrepresent my autism in my writing. I don't think I paint a particularly rosy portrait of our neurotype or our existence. My big, bold claims are that being autistic doesn't always entirely suck and that all autistic lives have value. I'm not exactly cagey about my own problems, either. I have stated that I have anxiety and depression, that I have hit myself and struggle with other repetitive movements that might lead to health issues. The extent to which

I rely on other people for support—and how much I worry about that—has been documented. I've brought up bullying, isolation, alienation, fear for the future and suicidal ideation. But I have chosen not to go into lurid detail on any of those topics, and that's a problem for some people.

When I publish anything on autism, I am inevitably greeted with a wave of emails, messages and comments from complete strangers—usually non-autistic parents of autistic children—accusing me of glamorizing autism because I don't talk about its hardships explicitly enough. Most of these messages include further questions about my own status. How old was I when I was toilet trained? Have I ever smeared feces on a wall? Do I hit myself? Have I hit others? How much of a burden was I to my parents growing up? Do I wear diapers? (If you're not autistic, you might think I'm exaggerating the obsession that people who don't know me have with my poop. If anything, I'm underselling the situation.)

At first I felt that I had to answer them. That maybe, if I elucidated my situation enough, they would realize that I was really autistic enough to have an opinion on my own life, and other lives like mine, in some way. That they would realize that I don't think that autism is a mere quirk or eccentricity, and that I have no interest in making other people believe it's that simple, either. Each time I tried, though, I was met with another round of dismissals and demands. There is nothing I can say, nothing I can expose, that will satisfy some people. You can strip yourself bare and still be accused of faking—of lying. Why would anyone want to do that to themselves? Why would anyone want them to?

Even now, as I write this, I'm struggling with the content and depth of my disclosures. This essay would flow better if I were to insert a personal anecdote right about now, for example. I'm aware that non-autistic people find it easier to connect with a topic when it's illustrated with casually recounted moments from the author's life. I don't *get* it, but it's a thing I'm willing to attempt for their comfort. Like small talk.

I really should give you a tangible example of an accusatory email I received, how I responded to it with the gory details of some of my most vulnerable moments, and how it was thrown back in my face. What's one more aside about the time I pooped my pants in grade three, the time I scrubbed my skin raw because I couldn't stand the smell of my own body or the time I accidentally smashed a mirror during a meltdown when most of those stories are already in the inboxes of strangers who demanded them with a fraction of the good faith that the average reader will likely bring to this book? But I think about how much it hurt to rip out those still-bleeding pieces of myself and hand them to someone else, and how much more it hurt to be told that they weren't bad or revelatory enough. And I can't muster the nerve to try again.

I would love to exist in a world where we could just be open about everything. In terms of self-interest, I would have so much mental energy left for other things if I didn't have to spend all of this time weighing what I can and can't safely say. And having a few internal crises over what that means. And perpetuating elaborate ruses to protect other people from any discomfort with my actual self, and protect myself from any actions they might take against me as a result. More altruistically, I believe that it would improve the quality of all autistic lives if we could eradicate the stigma surrounding what our brains and bodies do, and what and how they excrete. Erasing the shame that we place on needing support with those things would make a massive difference, too.

Until then, though, each autistic person—and the people who care about and for us—will have to negotiate what they feel safe sharing with others. I will continue to stumble around that fine line between sharing things that might make other people in my situation feel less alone and not saying anything that might make a future employer or nosey friend think twice about engaging with me if it came up in a Google search.

Whether it's the actual identity of your crush or the gory details of your latest meltdown, the dilemma is the same. You have no control over how the world will receive it, or what they'll do with it. Even the people who are trying to help can make mistakes (as far as I can tell, my friends were actually trying to set me up with D during that fated art class). Sometimes the only thing in your power is what you hide and how you hide it.

STEP FOUR

Make yourself useful

I SPENT MOST OF HIGH SCHOOL IN MY ROOM.

This is not hyperbole employed for tragicomic effect; it's a statistical fact. I was homeschooled for grades ten through twelve and I did the bulk of my work in my room. I had few friends during that period, and the ones that I had were usually busy with their normal lives and classmates, so I spent a lot of my free time there as well. Outside of a three-month co-op placement, some family visits and the rare social expedition, I had no real cause to leave it. I literally spent the majority of my high school years hanging out with a stuffed dinosaur[21] between four peach walls plastered with images of snarky musicians, oddly handsome supermarionettes and dead film legends.

I'd had an abysmal grade nine experience. My school board's gifted program ended in elementary school, so, after three years of relative peace in a class with other weirdos, I was tossed back into regular classes. I didn't live in the same school catchment as the friends I had made during that time, so I was ripped away from them ... and put right back with

....
21 My childhood favourite, Bluebell, who would be quite insulted if he didn't get a shout-out of some sort in this book.

the very bullies I'd joined the program to escape. They were not as vicious the second time around, but I never got any less afraid of them. About a third of the way through the year, I developed the absolutely genius idea that maybe the rejection of my peers would hurt less if I pushed them away first, so I became a bitter, cantankerous loner who quickly realized that alienation fucking sucks no matter what the cause of it is.

The only saving grace in this situation was that I was finally in the same school with my best friend[22] for the first time since we'd met in nursery school. But then she befriended my old bullies and I lost my mind and sobbed for a week straight, communicating my feelings almost entirely in Bob Mould lyrics. She knew what I'd been through with them. She'd been to that infamous eleventh birthday party. And she chose them. Everyone had warned me that boys would come and go; no one had prepared me for the possibility that friends could, too.

I wasn't left entirely alone by the platonic breakup. I could sometimes convince the girl who lived across the street to watch TV with me, and I still had two friends from my gifted years. But they had their own social circles and things going on. Their phone calls were intermittent and the plans we made subject to cancellation. Which felt a lot like being all alone to an angstier-than-average teenager.

I was almost as angry at the world as I was at myself. Everything felt hopeless. I'd worked so hard to be something less than hated for so many years and it had all fallen

....

22 This is the aforementioned one friend I managed to make and keep during my childhood. We met on the first day of nursery school. The first thing I told my parents when I went home was that I had a new best friend. For ten years—two-thirds of my life at that time—that was true. And then one day it wasn't. If I've gone light on details, that's because I don't believe our history or my loss bears any significance on my story beyond this mention of it. The breakup sucked and unmoored me, but now I can honestly say that she's just a footnote in my life.

apart. And I just couldn't envision a future where this pattern wouldn't repeat itself until one of my haters—be it me or someone equally sick of me—put me out of my misery. It was the kind of year that made pulling your daughter out of school and letting her spend a substantial chunk of her formative years alone in her room listening to copious amounts of Joy Division[23] the responsible parenting choice.

This period might sound pathetic on paper. I'm not going to argue that it was anything other than the least cool phase of a deeply uncool existence. But it really wasn't that bad. I was so burnt-out from trying to be some semblance of a real person, and so petrified of other humans, that I welcomed the chance to curl up in my bunker and regroup for a while. And it's amazing how much you can accomplish when you're young, overly intense and have no silly distractions like friends or a life to get in your way.

I read a ton and wrote almost as much. As far as I can tell, I became the sole patron of my local Blockbuster's foreign film rack, and devoured all of the Italian surrealism and Scandinavian depression it could offer me. My budding obsession with indie rock further intensified, and I plowed through a pretty impressive amount of self-reflection. Normal kids might have had things like experiences to learn and grow from, but I had a diary, endless hours of introspection and heroic doses of Ingmar Bergman at my disposal.

Removed from the constant psychological warfare and ongoing misery that I'd faced in the traditional school system, I had a little bit of space to start figuring out who I was, as opposed to who I thought I had to be. She really wasn't that terrible: weird as shit, but increasingly okay with that. An excitable nerd intensely into the things she loved. Pretty

....
23   Formed in 1976 and disbanded in 1980 when lead singer Ian Curtis died by suicide, Joy Division were Manchester's saddest post-punk goths. Which is saying a lot for a city that also produced The Smiths.

high on people who didn't suck, too. Socially and physically awkward, but trying her best. Bisexual (thanks, Mrs. Emma Peel and mid-afternoon reruns of *The Avengers* on Bravo!). A tender-hearted dork with a viciously sarcastic self-defence mechanism ... and the overly defensive instincts of a particularly dickish cat. Self-aware enough to realize that she'd replaced her anemic self-esteem with a fragile ego, and working on it, really. Anxious, melancholy and two-thirds convinced that the only people who understood her were an aging Swedish filmmaker and a dead Mancunian singer.

And lonely. I appreciated—and needed—my makeshift cocoon, but I also desperately wanted—and needed—something or someone to be out there for me as I started to emerge from it. I loved my parents and genuinely enjoyed their company (Mom was and remains my favourite concert companion), but they couldn't be the only people in my life. I wanted people I could cry and laugh with, share memories and inside jokes. I wanted to go to malls and movie theatres. I wanted to get invited to parties and maybe even work up the nerve to go once or twice.

To accomplish that, I was going to need a new plan of attack. Being myself was still, unfortunately, out. I was starting to like me, but I'd also established that I was a girl of obscure tastes, so I couldn't really count on anyone else being on board. My earlier method was also out now that I recognized its two glaring flaws: 1. No matter how hard I tried, the normals seemed to smell the not normal on me; and 2. I always seemed to hit a point where I resented the failing effort that I was putting into all of that bullshit and morphed into a snarky contrarian who wanted to set everything on fire.

So I came up with an even more genius and not at all self-destructive idea: If I couldn't or wouldn't blend in, I'd have to make having a complete fucking weirdo around worth someone's while. And if I couldn't make them value me as I was, I'd have to figure out how to make myself valuable to them.

This campaign began organically enough with my remaining friends. When they did call to check in, they'd naturally dominate the conversation because I never really had much to report. This would sometimes include their friend and boy troubles. I had little experience with either, but I could provide a sympathetic ear and be a safe sounding board. They knew how much time I'd spent observing other people from the sidelines and obsessively picking apart human interactions, and they figured this could give a unique and valuable outside perspective. So they started coming to me for advice. (They were mostly right. For someone who couldn't help herself to save her life, I sure had a lot of surprisingly useful suggestions for others. A few of those nuggets of wisdom were barely disguised digressions about *Kids in the Hall* skits. But nobody's perfect.)

I didn't mind being a confidante. I did genuinely care about my friends and it felt great to be able to help them in some way. Being able to provide a useful service for them also made me feel like I was properly earning their friendship. Somewhat less altruistically, I realized that they probably had to keep me around now, because I knew their secrets. I had no intention of exposing them, but maybe they didn't need to know that for sure.

One of those friends occasionally assured me that I could always come to her if I ever needed to talk. I'd thank her and tell her I appreciated the offer—and I was touched by her efforts each time—but insist that I didn't have that much going on. Sometimes that was true. Mostly I saw no point in trying to explain what I was going through to a relatively normal teenager. "I spend all of my time alone in a room hopped up on a multimedia celebration of existential dread and I am absolutely terrified that I am wasting the so-called best years of my life, but I don't know how to change any of that and the thought that the rest of my existence could all be downhill from *this* keeps me up at night more than my chronic sleep issues" wasn't exactly something they could help me with. And why risk making myself that raw to another person when the very best they could offer in return was pity? Besides, I dreaded tipping the scales in our relationships. Needing them more than they needed me could be disastrous.

I soon extended my new exceedingly accommodating spirit to our other interactions. If we were planning an outing, I figured as long as we stuck to stuff that appealed to them, they wouldn't question the necessity of taking me along. I'd already established that I had weird taste, so it was just easier to defer to them each time. "I'm good with anything, why don't you decide?" and "I don't know, what do you want to do?" became my default stances on any and all plan making. Eventually, I stopped offering much in the way of differing opinions at all. I only faltered and slid into contrarian dick mode when it came to music. The raging rock snob in me was already too stubborn.

The half cypher, half surrogate therapist routine allowed me to keep the friends I had, but it was doing little to expand my world, so I decided that more research and more drastic measures were in order. This impulse somehow led to me making what I still consider the worst choice of my life: turning to the internet.

These days, we all know that the internet is a terrible extension of our terrible world, but in the late nineties it still seemed promising to a somewhat naive loner with few other options. At the very least, it was a more welcoming and less potentially abusive place than my hometown. So I started spending a lot of time there. The decision wasn't a complete wash. I did stumble onto a few music message boards and meet some like-minded nerds to chat with. But my new genius plan wasn't to make friends; it was to conduct extensive research into how to make myself as worthy of those friends as possible.

General advice on the subject wasn't going to cut it for me. Most lonely teenagers are simply told to be themselves, and assured that true friends will appreciate them for it. I already knew that tactic was for other people, so I had to keep looking. When the search for tips on what to do was getting me nowhere, I switched my focus to figuring out what not to do. The politeness of normal society doesn't allow people to directly state what they want out of each other ... but it does allow them to sneak off to semi-anonymous online forums to viciously bitch about the ways in which their fellow human beings have failed to live up to their unstated standards.

I started reading every advice and etiquette column I could find, not for the content of the articles, but for the comment section. That was where I could access a wide variety of unfiltered opinions on every aspect of human interaction from what kind of gifts people dislike (everything except money ... and money can be considered tacky), to traits people dislike in a woman (everything). I once read an entire discussion thread dedicated to how much the numerous posters involved *hated* it when a woman played with her hair, which was illuminating and alarming to me as a lifelong hair twiddler.[24]

Celebrity gossip message boards were another favourite resource of mine, because most of what commenters say about stars are just exaggerated projections of their everyday opinions. Through a thread on Britney Spears's speaking voice, I could gain insight into how people interpreted pitch

....
24 Hair twirling is my most common stim.

and pacing in verbal conversation. A discussion on Kirsten Dunst exposed me to the wide variety of off-putting characteristics and moral failings that people can and will read into body language like a slight slouch. And all of the topics involving female celebrities taught me that women really can't do anything right.

This seething cesspool of plainly stated rage felt like a goldmine to me. For so many years, I'd wished I could have known what my classmates were saying behind my back, or that they would just tell me what I was doing wrong. And now I had access to the whole world's id.

I truly believed that I could use this raw material to help me identify my extensive flaws, and chip away at them until all that was left was an infallible person who wouldn't cause any distaste, discomfort or mild annoyance to others. Which would make me valuable to them. I tried to stop playing with my hair and, when that didn't work, cut it too short to twirl. Then I turned my focus to my voice, posture, physical mannerisms, gift-giving, kneecaps and my everything else. Even after I began to realize that it was impossible to eradicate every little thing anyone might dislike—because people, especially when they're anonymous on the internet, can and will hate everything[25]—I still tried. And I hated myself for failing ... and for all of the new glaring flaws I'd noticed as a result of my studies.

Two decades and what I hope is a shred of maturity later, I can look back at my methodology with a wincing laugh. But I still understand—and feel—the impulse behind my actions.

....

25. There are people who think kneecaps can be ugly! I learned this from a very detailed and very angry discourse about Beyoncé's legs. And if Beyoncé's patellas aren't good enough for the internet, what hope is there for the rest of us?

From casual conversation to life-or-death medical decisions, our society consistently ties the value of a disabled
person's life to the value we provide—or fail to provide—to
abled people. Parents and partners of disabled human beings
are praised and pitied for how hard they must work, how
hard we must be on their time, their emotions and their sav-
ings. Most art involving disability is still about how abled
people were challenged by, how they survived and what they
learned from taking care of us and/or loving us. Something
as simple as the common fears that parents express when
their child is diagnosed with autism can revolve around these
themes. It's not even about what we may or may not be able
to share; it's about what we can't offer. "I'm afraid I'll never
hear my child say 'I love you'" is a common refrain. "I'm
afraid I'll never know that my child loves me" or "I'm afraid
that my child will never know that they are loved" are not.

Throughout our lives, disabled people watch abled folk
calculate our risk vs. benefit. Are we a drain on public and
personal resources? Does it cost too much, both emotionally
and financially, to bring us into this world and keep us here?
Does it cost too much money to house us, educate us, feed us
or help us access the supports that can help us lead healthier
and more fulfilling lives? Are we too much of a burden on
the people who love us, on the social system or the environment? When, if ever, will we be able to support ourselves
and become contributing members of society, whatever that
means? Who's going to pay for it if we don't?

As I write this, the hashtag #PayNowOrPayLater is gaining traction in Ontario. It's a response to changes that our
provincial government wants to make to the current funding model for autistic children. It's a complicated situation,
far too nuanced for the level of discussion that can happen
on Twitter or in the course of the average person's political
engagement. The proposed changes are bad, but the funding

that did exist was already broken and failed the autistic population both in terms of the number of people it helped and the variety of services it offered. In fighting to protect autistics and their families, perfectly well-meaning people are rejecting any conversations about what treatments and supports will actually help us and are virulently fighting for the status quo. This complicated situation has been further grossly simplified into the basic argument behind this hashtag: Autistic children who are denied services now will become a bigger burden on the health care system as they age. The people who are trying to be on our side have reduced us to a mere calculation.

Even in death, the tab isn't settled. Fear of becoming a burden to loved ones is a common motivator for people who seek assisted suicide.[26] Our absence is considered a relief. If one of us is the victim of filicide, we're asked to sympathize with the killers and how hard life must have been for them. It's just accepted that whatever we bring to their lives in return is not enough to offset our cost in the end.

Sometimes I make progress—plodding, non-linear progress—on the ways in which I try to make myself valuable to people. But that desperate, all-encompassing *need* to make myself useful, and the even more desperate feeling that I'm failing at it, have yet to budge.

In the years following my eventual autism diagnosis, my therapist and I spent a lot of time talking about my message board fixation. We tried weaning me off of them. We tried quitting cold turkey. I kept going back to them, so he kept

....

26 The fact that autism has been cited in assisted death cases in Belgium and the Netherlands is never far from my mind when I'm feeling low. The CBC provided a good overview of the situation in the 2019 article "The Next Frontier in the 'Right to Die': Advance Requests, Minors and the Mentally Ill" (https://www. cbc.ca/news/politics/maid-assisted-death-minors-mental-illness-1.4956388). You can also search for the terms "autism" and "assisted death" for more information, as I have many times.

going back to why I thought I needed them. I told him that I consciously knew I would never find any useful information about how be worthy of others in anonymous bile spilled over celebrities, but I didn't know what else to do. That as long as I felt like I had to make up for who I was and what I couldn't be or provide, I'd look anywhere for cues on how to pay back that debt. Including the very message boards that once inspired me to spend months trying to come up with new methods for brushing my hair off my face ... because two posters thought that Jennifer Aniston's method made her look bitchy.

"Have you ever considered that your worth doesn't come from your work, or what you can do for other people?" he asked.

"No," I grumbled, genuinely confused by whatever bonkers thought experiment he was trying to put me through. "Where the fuck else would it come from?"

"You have worth because you're a person," he replied.

I glared somewhere in his general eye region and laughed. I considered walking out and quitting. Why was I wasting my time and money working under the guidance of someone who could spout such lofty idealism with a straight face? How was I supposed to get anywhere in our ugly, dystopian nightmare world with a therapist who was dealing in daydreams?

I don't disagree with the sentiment. If you get me in a righteous social justice mood, I will tell you that we should think of our human connections as something deeper than a basic bartering system. That people are more than what they can do for you, and you're more than what you can provide in return. And that anyone who actively participates in perpetuating a society where that isn't the case is a greater scourge on said society than any human being who needs anything from a little extra patience to 24/7 care could ever be. If I'm among feminists, I might add that the messages

I receive about being a burden as a disabled person aren't entirely unlike the messages I receive about being high maintenance as a woman. Find me in earnest spirits and I'll say that a perfectly balanced ledger isn't always the same thing as a mutually rewarding relationship and there are so many immeasurable ways we can make each other's lives better just by being in them.[27] I genuinely believe all of the above is true ... for everyone not named Sarah Jane Kurchak.

I have first-hand experience with the fallout of chasing companionship at the expense of selfhood. Three years into my bedroom-based social experiment, I said a bit too much about my own worries in a phone call with my friend. "What problems could you ever have?" she replied. A few months after that, I listened to a male acquaintance I'd started hanging out with at my work co-op describe me to a third party, and it dawned on me that he was only describing himself.

I've since realized that the latter scenario is not uncommon for a certain type of person (i.e., solipsistic dudes), but I didn't really blame either of them. They may have been callous or self-interested, but their actions weren't exactly uncalled for when I'd put so much effort into cultivating the illusion that I wasn't different from them in any way. That didn't make it sting any less, though. There's a whole new crushing loneliness that comes with being allowed in the room but remaining unseen. I'm also lucky enough to know

....

27 Then I'll probably launch into an extended monologue about an episode of the 2019 stop-motion animation series *Rilakkuma and Kaoru* because I never really got over that whole giving-TV-based-advice thing. And because the episode is a genuinely thoughtful and kind take on the topic: Rilakkuma, an adorable but clumsy bear, tries to get a job to help contribute to his household but keeps getting fired. Demoralized, he tells his family that they should eat him instead. His human, Kaoru, suggests that he would taste terrible and is better suited to helping her stay warm at night. We all learn an important lesson about everybody contributing what they can in their own way. And I have a perfectly normal sob over a cartoon bear as I push forty.

what the alternative to that emptiness feels like now. I've met people who see my value and forged relationships rooted in mutual respect and affection.

But I still struggle to take any of it to heart. That's how overwhelming the messages that disabled people receive about our value are. That's how deep the fear runs.

I sometimes joke that my only savant-like skill is the ability to keep running calculations of what I contribute to my loved ones versus what I take from them. But it's not really a joke. I keep tabs on everything from how balanced my conversations are to how much my parents continue to invest in me. I worry that believing people won't give up on me because they accept and value me as I am is just a cop out, and that I need to try even harder to be worthy of their efforts. The insecurities never fade. When I finish my tabulations each night, I'm always a little in the red.

STEP FIVE

Work and socialize with people who are arguably less normal than you are

IF YOU HAPPEN TO HAVE INTENSE INTERESTS, RIGID AND REPETI-tive behaviours and a neurobehavioral condition that involves issues with social interaction, and you're in the market for a workplace where your myriad foibles might not be quite so glaring, there are worse places you could end up than a music magazine.

I did not take an internship at the now dearly departed *Chart* magazine in Toronto in the hope of finding my people or some approximation thereof. I wish I could say that it was an idea born of that kind of self-awareness and optimism. In reality, I was a mildly naive eighteen-year-old who had limited resources and perspective but boundless creative logic at her disposal.

This was painfully clear in my thought process: After three years of homeschooling, I was bored and even sicker of my crappy hometown than usual. I wanted to be in Toronto. University was the obvious choice, and probably the good choice, to get me there, but I didn't see how I could afford that. I was terribly afraid of student loan debt, and burning out of the regular school system blew most of the scholarship hopes that a once promising student of my nature might have had. But writing wasn't like medicine or law, was it? Maybe I didn't really need a formal education to learn how to do it, or start doing it. So maybe I could try an internship and then reconsider my post-secondary options the next year. (That I never went back is a tragic story about class, not a tragic story about autism.)

I'd never once expressed a dash of interest in journalism, but I obsessively loved Canadian music and *Chart* magazine, and I figured writing was writing, so I started with them. The good people of *Chart* were working in a dying and disenfranchised industry that covered another dying and disenfranchised industry, *in Canada*, so they were in no position to turn down the free labour of a moderately feral weirdo. It was a match made in, well, Canadian music.

I did not go straight from my bedroom to *Chart*. A distant relative helped land me a place at the sci-fi TV station Space that I used for co-op credits at the end of my homeschooling period. I spent a few months crashing with my grandparents at their midtown Toronto apartment, fetching coffee, filing and doing my best to reintegrate into the world. It wasn't a terrible experience, and I managed not to screw up. My hard work and determination earned positive attention, and I got to meet Buzz Aldrin. There was just nothing that I accomplished during my time there that gave me any indication that real life wasn't just as mercenary, scary and completely outside of my skill set as high school. I was still awkward and strange, still missing cues and feeling like I was on a thirty-second (or thirty-minute) delay from everyone around me. I still thought that tolerance might be the best I could hope for.

I don't mean to shrug off such a major experience. "Oh yeah, I went from being homeschooled in a small town to having a work placement at a national cable station, here's a whole paragraph on it!" likely makes me sound blasé and spoiled. The opportunity was a massive privilege. The circumstances surrounding it were a big deal, too. I went straight from running away from childhood bullies to leaping into a workplace culture so notoriously Machiavellian that it's frequently satirized in its own medium. That's pretty damned significant.

When I look back at the ass end of my formative years, though, it's my twelve-month internship at *Chart* (which grew into ten years of freelancing for the magazine and website) that really does feel like the start of my life.

That life did not begin auspiciously. On my first day there, I managed to get lost travelling from Queen Street East to Queen Street West (a.k.a. going in a straight line), get caught in a rainstorm and collapse into a sobbing fit on a streetcar in the course of a simple errand run. The only thing that kept me from completely melting down in fear of being fired was my budding plan to quit. But I wasn't, so I didn't, and I was greeted with a less nightmarish day two.

Mild humiliation aside, the first thing I noticed about my new internship was how relatively easy the conversation felt. I was still a fumbling dork—I suspect I always will be—but this no longer seemed like a massive stumbling block. My new officemates just ... kept talking to me. About subject matter that I understood, cared about and could contribute to. Even the majority of the office's small talk was in my wheelhouse.

My introductions to each staff member were variations on this theme:

Them: What kind of music do you like?

Me: The Lowest of the Low. Change of Heart. The Weakerthans. Rough Trade. I just bought a couple of Hüsker Dü records.

Them: Oh, Hüsker Dü! Which album is your favourite?

Me: I'm supposed to say *Zen Arcade*, aren't I? But ... I love *Flip Your Wig*.

Them: Actually, I prefer *Flip Your Wig*, too.

This dialogue sounds like a weak *High Fidelity* parody to me now, but at the time it was the makings of some of the smoothest conversations I'd had with anyone not directly involved in my creation. It felt comfortable, almost intuitive. I was so excited that I could keep up (and honestly relieved that there were other people out there who didn't wholeheartedly buy into the cult of *Zen Arcade*). Soon, I stopped panicking when I was called on to contribute. Then I started looking forward to it. At some point, I began jumping into the wide-ranging discussions that floated across the small office of my own volition. And was welcomed into them.

The *Chart* office was by no means a cuddly environment. On the surface, it was probably more biting, sarcastic and rough around the edges than any other microcosm of humanity I'd been a part of. The people who worked there—and the large cast of freelancing misfits who wandered in for new assignments, gossip, arguments and bizarre in-jokes—were sharp-tongued and strident. They'd grown up treating three- to five-minute packets of misery and anger like a religion. Now dissecting, ranking, cataloguing and waxing poetic on these melodic cries for help was their calling. There really wasn't any hope for any of them blending into polite society.

Polite and kind can be quite different things, though. Even my bullies had managed to be nice to my face, for a while. After what I'd been through, and how I'd coped, I wasn't particularly in the mood for nice anymore, anyway. The music writers and editors I met during this period could be uncouth, but only a few of them were truly bad people. Under most of those abrasive exteriors lurked a good-hearted nerd looking for the same.[28] Many of them had been through some shit they didn't want to repeat. They had defence mechanisms where their social skills should be, but they'd somehow managed to MacGyver their favourite tools of defence—sarcasm, burns, copious Smiths lyrics—into a means of bonding. These sweet and tender hooligans weren't exactly *like me*, but they were close enough. They took me in like a litter of cats adopting an orphaned squirrel.

I've only become slightly less prickly with age, and the cynic in me is leery of overstating the importance of finding your people in life. A true sense of community doesn't entirely fix anything. It can't cure everything. No autistic person, not even a so-called "mild" one, will see all of their needs magically disappear if they're lucky enough to stumble into the right subculture. Making meaningful connections can't eradicate sensory issues and repetitive behaviours, nor can such bonds completely heal whatever wounds you accrued while still searching for them.

I have also become far more earnest—or perhaps more comfortable with how earnest I secretly was all along—with age, though, and I refuse to sell the power of belonging short. Being around supportive, like-minded people can drastically improve your life. In addition to helping you survive, it can make you want to. If you've lived without that feeling for any period of time, if you've had to fight to find it, the sense of no longer being alone in the world can be transformative. Whether it's the Island of Misfit Toys,[29] or Tetsuya Naito

....
28 Hi, Erik.
29 The refuge where imperfect and unwanted toys find and support each other in the beloved 1964 TV special *Rudolph the Red-Nosed Reindeer.*

assembling Los Ingobernables de Japon,[30] there's a reason why stories about loners and outsiders finding each other and finding a new future through each other resonate so deeply with audiences. It's because they're true.

Getting my first taste of place and purpose didn't just make me *feel like* life was possible for the first time, it actually started to make that life possible. Tackling your myriad issues becomes a lot more feasible when you're not living under constant threat of exclusion—or worse. I still struggled with the same things that had always challenged me. I said weird things, mostly unintentionally. Basic navigation of the city I was born in remained an elusive goal. The most random and seemingly harmless circumstances could catch me completely off guard and overwhelm me in ways I couldn't always understand or express. The way that I was able to handle all of these things changed, though. Once I was relatively secure that the bottom wouldn't fall out each time I made a mistake, my brain and body stopped responding with such brutal anxious immediacy every time I did. I didn't panic quite as much. My thought process didn't spiral so quickly or deeply out of control. Which meant that I wasn't always at risk of a full-blown meltdown. This left me with all sorts of energy that I'd never had before to work through my reactions, my fears and my options. There's incredible power in having some sort of margin of error in which to live and learn.

There's also immense power in working toward something you care about, as opposed to acting out of fear. I'd wanted to be a writer since kindergarten and I'd been deeply

....

30   LIJ are a stable of six professional wrestlers in New Japan Pro Wrestling who have, for various reasons, been misunderstood or overlooked in their pasts. Nominally led by ungovernably haired and puppy dog–eyed iconoclast Naito, this egalitarian brotherhood of absolute goth units, space pirates, well-manicured masked men, mulleted muscle men and weirdo genius cat-loving artists who can talk to inanimate objects has united to offer each other support and (mostly) friendly competition. And generally be the coolest people alive.

invested in indie rock and its various permutations for most of my adolescence. Interning at a music magazine gave me a chance to combine a craft that I had been carefully honing for most of my life with a very intense interest of mine. I was engaged and excited. Within that context, a lot of behaviours and social skills that I'd written off as useless, or in some way beyond my knowledge or ability, took on new meaning. The difference between "I need to figure out how to perfectly execute this social function before someone kicks my locker or maybe my head in" and "figuring out how to perform this function would improve my ability to interview artists, and interact with my fellow music critics" can be the difference between "this is futile and I might as well die" and "I am going to try."

Reciprocal conversation, for example, had always been a major stumbling block for me. It's not that I didn't care about what other people were doing or thinking, I just couldn't wrap my head around the necessity of asking them specific things to demonstrate that interest. My ideal conversation would be an exchange of interconnected statements. One person could initiate by bringing up an idea or point that they thought another person could be interested in. The second person could then relate their own ideas or points to those initial statements. The first person could bounce further sentences that were punctuated with periods and the occasional exclamation mark off of that, and so forth. As I have been repeatedly informed, though, this fails to convey proper investment to most other parties. Apparently it can make you sound self-absorbed and aloof. I tried to remedy my natural conversational style for years, but could not properly wrap my head around finding the right things to ask, putting them into the proper words and then making my voice appropriately rise at the end of those assembled words. My awkwardly crafted and even more awkwardly worded questions stopped conversations almost as dead as my lack of them had.

When my editors started assigning me interviews, questions suddenly became more of a necessity than ever. But they also immediately started making more sense. An interview is a pretty formalized social structure, where each person involved has a certain role. If you're interviewing someone, it's your job to draw answers out of them. You can occasionally get away with a statement that could inspire further reflection, but most of what you will need to say to drive the conversation and achieve its desired ends are questions. When you begin an interview, you usually have a more structured idea of what you need to discuss than you would in a casual conversation. If you're able to read other interviews with your subject as part of your preparation, you might also have an idea of what will come up and how it will be discussed. From there, it's relatively easy to figure out what you will need to ask to do your job well. If you're still not sure, well, you will usually have plenty of time to think the issues over, rewrite and rehearse. You can even use notes during the actual talking part!

Once the concept, development and execution of questions started to make more sense to me, I was able to start experimenting with them in less rigid settings. Mutually invested statement-based conversations are still my ideal, and I think they get a bad rap, but I can now hold my own in a reciprocal situation to keep the normals happy, thanks to this process.

Transcribing those interviews gave me valuable insight into a lot of other aspects of verbal communication, too. I hated having to listen to my own voice and winced through what always sounded like terrible questions in retrospect. (This might be the worst part of pop culture journalism, outside of the borderline poverty. I've yet to meet a single colleague who remotely enjoys the experience.) But it did give me a chance to go over my performance the way an athlete reviews game tape. I was able to observe the tone and melody of my voice, the flow of my speech patterns and the efficacy of my questions. I could make note of what sounded too awkward, too flat, too up-talky and too fast. Then I would practice different phrases, paces and sounds to see what might work better. My interview subjects—mostly charismatic and beloved performers—also provided excellent study material. Through talking to them, and then re-listening to them speak, and then typing out the words they'd used, I started to develop a better sense of what connects with audiences and why.

I tried my best to apply what I'd learned to my own interactions. I tried even harder to give myself a break for the things I probably couldn't change. On rare occasions, I even came to accept that my seemingly inherent awkwardness had some surprise benefits. I hated that strange, slightly too long pause I took to regroup between a subject's answer and my next question until I realized that it served the same function as a trained journalist's pregnant pause.

While makeshift social skills lessons like these helped me to work on some things that were within my control, being around my colleagues and fledgling friends helped me to accept things that maybe weren't. Sure, I was still immutably weird in so many ways, but so were they. These people didn't just tolerate my many foibles; they had an assload of their own. Within that bubble, parts of myself that I'd long considered massive deficits no longer seemed like the end of the world. I may have been the only autistic person in the loose-knit community of music writers that I got to know through *Chart*—although that's debatable—but I was never the strangest or least capable of regular human functions.

I don't suggest this glibly. As I've said, I'm not the type to argue that autism is merely a quirk or the next step in human evolution. I don't believe that acceptance alone would be enough to entirely address the needs that we have as a result of our neurology. However, there's nothing quite like immersing yourself in a culture of obsessive pedants with rigorous filing processes and meticulous records and rankings to make you realize that sometimes the line between dedicated and disordered isn't always clear. There's nothing like being welcomed into such a world to make you reconsider what you really needed to change in your life: Was it just yourself, or was it also your audience?

I believe the way that we currently talk about social issues in the autistic population is grossly oversimplified. Yes, we struggle with them—many of us quite severely—and can suffer great repercussions as a result. It's a serious problem. But it is a matter much bigger than our own flaws. There are always other factors involved, from the behaviour and taste of the people around us to the conventions of the culture in which we're interacting. If our solutions only address one aspect of this complex situation, we're really not doing anything to make autistic lives safer or more fulfilling. Learning and regurgitating someone else's often arbitrary rules of engagement doesn't guarantee that those people will grant you base level tolerance in return. Nor does it guarantee that you'll find anything of value in the connections that you do make this way.

I don't assume that what helped me would work for everyone. (Even if signing every autistic person up for an internship in music journalism was a solution, it's not like there are any outlets left, anyway.) I don't know if finding an equivalent application for another autistic person's special interest will pay off the same way mine did. And I am definitely not going to tell you that there's a secret genius hiding inside of every autistic person, just waiting to be sparked by the right subject matter. Falling into the community I did at *Chart* wasn't the only help I needed, either. This book isn't called *I Interned at a Nerd-Riddled Workplace Geared to My Intense Interests and Everything's Been Great Since Then.* But something doesn't need to fix your life to transform it.

Seeing some of your greatest gains come from an unlikely source is the kind of experience that can make a person wonder what else might be possible for people like them. If most of my conscious efforts to fix myself and my social skills were painful failures compared to this potentially ill-advised misadventure, what other happy accidents and dipshit discoveries could be out there? What tools for greater acceptance and integration might we be missing when society is working from such a narrow concept of the social problems that autistic people face? What small breaths of relief and hints of a better future are we ignoring when we only look for solutions or cures?

STEP SIX

Make the worst possible choices in love. Somehow meet the right person anyway

WHEN NON-AUTISTIC PARENTS OF AUTISTIC CHILDREN APPROACH me about autism, the conversation usually goes one of two ways: they ask me about my toilet training or they ask me about my life.

The former see me as an imposter trying to usurp attention from their child's real problems. Their questions are posed with the intent to expose me as a pretender, to prove that I can't possibly be autistic enough to be taken seriously as an autistic person.

The latter see a potential future for their children in me. They're asking because they want examples of what might be possible: Do I live independently? Work? What do I do? How am I doing? Am I seeing someone? It's the last one they ask most anxiously. It's my answer to this question that seems to bring them the most comfort.

I suppose it's possible that they respond this way because my marriage is the only solid evidence of my adulthood I can offer them. No parent who is already nervous about what might happen to their child after they're gone can take much solace in the idea that said offspring could grow up to be a freelance writer renting in an overpriced city, after all. But I think their relief runs deeper than that. My love life seems to be proof that their child isn't doomed to be alone.

I empathize with the impulse. These parents love their children and they want nothing more than for others to love and care for them too. However I worry that attaching these desires specifically to romantic love—particularly old-fashioned heteronormative signifiers of romantic love— is misguided. Not all autistic people are interested in sex and/or love. Not all of us who are consider it our primary goal. Getting hitched doesn't guarantee that you'll be cared for. People can feel alone in a marriage. Others can be thoroughly supported by the platonic love in their lives. Some people are happy alone.

And some people are happily married but mortifyingly aware of how many bullets they blithely dodged to wind up this way. Which makes them leery of being treated as any sort of positive example when it comes to matters of the heart and loins.

I became aware that boys didn't like me almost immediately after I became aware of boys. I don't recall it being much of a shock. If no one wanted to be my friend, then it stood to reason that no one would want to be my more-than-friend either. It still sucked, though. Watching the girls who had rejected me openly crush on people and successfully act on those crushes—and watching boys loudly profess their clumsy budding horndog appreciation for them in return—left me even more isolated. Their growing feelings were becoming a source of excitement and discovery while mine seemed to be turning into yet another source of humiliation. Whenever I betrayed any interest in someone, they responded with disgust or something even worse: pity. This could then be used as source material for further bullying. With a mix of pragmatism and great melodrama, I concluded that love was, like most things, for other people. I resigned myself to a life of silently pining for classmates, cartoon Ghostbusting nerds and ninja turtles. (When all romance seems hypothetical to you, being attracted to cartoons feels no less feasible than being attracted to humans.)

This exile was briefly disrupted by a pair of courtships at twelve and sixteen that started awkwardly and ended miserably, but were sort of okay while they lasted. The boys didn't particularly set any part of me on fire, but they liked me and I was excited by this novelty. Then they moved on and I returned to the unrequited status quo. I couldn't even get someone to hold my hand between the ages of sixteen and nineteen.

I know loneliness, romantic rejection and sexual frustration aren't easy for anyone. It can be particularly hurtful if you're outside of the norm in any way. Yet another reminder of how you don't belong, how you're lesser and undeserving. Yet another piece of mounting evidence your insecurities have assembled to prove that nothing will ever get better. Relentlessly experiencing those things as a teenage girl is a special kind of mindfuck, though. For as long as I could remember, family, teachers, sex ed nurses and pop culture had hammered it into my head that boys only wanted one thing. I was taught how to respect myself, how to demand that respect from potential romantic partners, how to say no and how to wait. And I was good with those concepts. They were actually some of the more sensible, straightforward social lessons that I received in my youth: Don't do things with people who don't respect you, don't do things you don't want to and don't let anyone pressure you into something you don't want to do. I was so ready to apply them when the time came! When that time never arrived, though, I started to develop a bit of a complex. Especially when I realized that I had, in fact, been raring to say yes for quite some time. Do you know how incredibly demoralizing it is to be told that boys will fuck anything—including, according to one popular movie released at the peak of my humiliation, a pie—when they will not fuck you? Do you have any idea how frantically that makes you question every aspect of your body and being?

I was extremely insecure about my looks (I still am, to the point where it can trigger meltdowns and I should really talk to a professional about body dysmorphic disorder) but I knew that my homeliness alone wasn't to blame. Although I started joking that my personality was more effective than any chastity belt, I think a part of me was aware that my abrasive exterior wasn't the only issue, either.

The bigger issue was that neither skill nor circumstance was on my side. I didn't know how to talk to boys, and I had a deep—and completely justified—fear of rejection. Not feeling like I could risk outright telling a boy I liked him or asking him out meant that I had to rely on subtle cues and hints that he might be into me before attempting anything. And, as we've already established, I couldn't do that to save my life. The whole homeschooling thing also drastically limited my access to boys. I also liked girls but, far from doubling my options, bisexuality only made my situation more tragic. I lived in a small and not exactly progressive town. No one was out. Whatever the closeted queer girls of the Niagara Region were doing to find each other was beyond my grasp, and so, therefore, were they.

I spent my adolescence bitterly horny and confused, pouting over songs about unrequited love and writing things like "I think this sexual frustration has turned to anger" in my melodramatic journal. I developed a fondness for hate-watching teen dramas like *My So-Called Life*, *Dawson's*

Creek and *Roswell* and taking it as a personal affront whenever any of the characters lost their virginity.

I blew the smattering of opportunities I stumbled into with wincingly comic cluelessness. My attempt to hit on a boy at a pool hall by quoting the scene from David Cronenberg's *Videodrome* where Max Renn and Nicki Brand flirt about Freud and the colour red brutally crashed and burned. An attempt to flirt with a different boy by making a joke about butter and *Last Tango in Paris* (I know. I'm genuinely horrified by my younger self now, too) during an improv seminar (I know. I'm genuinely horrified by my younger self now, too) was worse. It never occurred to me that they didn't get my references. It didn't actually occur to me that some nineties teenagers might have better things to do than obsessively brush up on their eighties body horror and seventies erotic drama at all, because isolation and hormones were starting to do a number on my perspective in general.

I thoroughly failed to recognize the possibility that the very pretty girl at the vintage store I regularly visited on lunch hours during my co-op might be making overtures when she told me that I should visit her regular café. And what days she usually went there. And her preference in underwear. A promising date and a half with cute curly-haired suitor went off the rails when he informed me that he had brought his fish back to life by shocking it with a nine-volt battery. I didn't know how to respond to that, so I just never responded to him again.

I spent my nineteenth birthday with my parents, waiting quietly until they were asleep (because I didn't want my *feelings* to hurt them or make me appear ungrateful for everything they did for me) to sob in the shower as I contemplated the rest of my lonely life. I cried so hard my abs ached the next day.

Then I hooked up with one of the editors at my internship and we lived happily ever after.

So you can see why I might be hesitant to be treated as any kind of role model when it comes to this stuff.

I want to be perfectly fucking clear before I continue: Do not, at any point during your internship, hook up with your superior. Who is ten years older than you. And going through a divorce.[31] Especially when you're not the most experienced or worldly nineteen-year-old on the planet. Do not take my story as an example that *you never know*, and/or *things have a way of working out*, no matter how terrible an idea might seem on paper. There is a 1 in 954,869,504,865,904,869,405, 869,045,869,045,896 chance that the above scenario will not end abysmally, and I am the horseshoes-hung fool who obtusely bumbled into that one. I do not endorse following in my footsteps. I cannot stress—and can't get over—how incredibly lucky I am that I did not risk my young career and heart for someone who turned out to be a manipulator, an abuser, a groomer, a selfish prick or even a run-of-the-mill dick.

I developed the first hints of a crush on Aaron on my second day at *Chart*. In the middle of editing my story, he got up, walked over to my desk and read a lightly snide line back to me. "We've got to keep an eye on you," he said in what I now know and love as his trademark deadpan tone.

Finally, someone gets it, I thought.

....

31 I wasn't a factor in the breakup of his first marriage at all, if you're curious. He was well into Ontario's protracted divorce proceedings when we started hanging out. I appreciate that relationships are complicated and try to approach other people's choices with nuance and compassion. I believe calling autistic people black and white thinkers is an oversimplification. But my personal moral code concerning affairs, including emotional ones, is autistically rigid.

I was smitten, but also cognizant of the fact that he was wearing a wedding ring, and I wouldn't let myself think about him *that way* as long as it was present.[32] When the ring disappeared and remained gone long enough to suggest that he hadn't simply misplaced it or forgotten it, though, I got properly moony-eyed very quickly. He was smart, witty and just a little strange. I found his elaborate ranking system of fast-food restaurants within a certain radius of the office bizarrely charming. Although he wasn't exactly like me, I felt like we might be from the same world. One of the first things Mom said after meeting him was, "He talks like you."

Aaron and I also liked many of the same things—*Dune*, music that was clever but miserable, being on the right side of the looming class war, each other—so we started hanging out as more than colleagues. We were both at a point in our lives where we were not actively looking or hoping for anything serious, but were equally uninterested in anything careless or empty, so we thought we'd have some respectful fun together. For a while, we did. At some point, we both somehow came to the conclusion that we wanted more, so we set about the awkward process of converting a fling into a potentially long-term relationship. And I began a bloody and legitimately terrifying but ultimately rewarding two-year process to win over his adorably murderous cat, Sable, with my unflagging affection.

Neither of us was exactly prepared or well equipped for this task. We were flailing gun-shy nerds who made mistakes and miscommunicated. We hurt each other, about 98 percent unintentionally. But we cared about each other and were

....
32 I wasn't kidding about that autistic moral rigidity.

invested in trying to build something together. My weird-ness gave him the space to be more fully himself, and his fractionally milder weirdness provided me with a level of stability and support that grounded me without restraining me. We worked at it, but we were also incredibly fortunate. Our love and combined efforts happened to align with our circumstances in a way that worked for us. Our challenges now, almost twenty years in, are mostly in line with what most long-term couples face: health issues, the deaths of loved ones, preparing for the looming class wars and various financial struggles. (While I'm doling out cautionary advice, might I also recommend not becoming a writer if you have any other options?) Our joys are, too.

I'm not saying that autism is no longer a big deal in my love life. It's a constant factor in my life in general, so of course it's a constant in my relationship, too. It has been a source of some serious arguments, including the one we had right after my diagnosis, which occurred eight years into our relationship. Aaron received it weirdly at first, in a way I couldn't quite interpret. Having celebrated my new-found awareness of myself by obsessively reading up on the myriad ways in which autism has been blamed for ruining relationships, I panicked and assumed that my own would be the next casualty. He assured me that wasn't the case, but went on to confess that he was afraid that I "might use it as an excuse."

Justifiably hurt and somewhat less justifiably snarky about this concern, I responded not by informing him that an explanation is not the same thing as an excuse. Or that it broke my heart a little to think that anyone who knew me as well as he did, who knew how fucking hard I was on myself, would ever think that I was suddenly going to use the one thing that made my life make a tiny bit more sense as a cheap out. Instead, I went straight to sarcastically blaming everything on my autism. If I spilled my tea? "Oh, I'm sorry. I have *autism*. I can't help it." Stubbed my toe? "Well, as you know, I stubbed my toe because I'm *autistic*." Or "Can you help me get this bowl from the top shelf? I can't reach it *because I have autism*." Two days into the incredibly mature campaign, we were able to have a proper talk with a real resolution to it. The issue has never resurfaced.

Some of our communication issues remain works in progress, like my tendency to ask him if he's mad at me. At least once a day. Aaron has never given me any cause to live in constant fear of his wrath. He can be almost as sarcastic as I am, but he's kind, and pretty forthcoming. He would tell me if he were upset. He has told me that he would tell me if he were upset. But I have lingering insecurities about my social skills, and I'm not immune to all of the tired, painful assumptions that I hear about autism ruining relationships. I regularly fear that I will do something terrible, fail to realize it and then fail to realize that he hates me for it. And that the situation will only degrade and decay until he finally frees himself from that clueless monster who ignored all of his pain/frustration/anger/etc.

The only thing I can do to pre-empt this seemingly inevitable disaster is to ask him if he's mad at me when he shows any signs of potential distress. Of course, I still struggle to read people properly. I'm more in tune with Aaron's thoughts and moods than most, but I did infamously respond to his proposal by looking at him as he kneeled and brandished a ring and earnestly asking if he was making fun of me. So almost everything looks like dismay or disappointment to me. Which means that the love of my life has heard the words "Are you mad at me?" every day for the past eighteen years of his existence.

For the first few years, he was patient. "Why would I be mad you?" he'd ask before kindly reassuring me that he would tell me if he were upset for any reason. Then the patience evolved into a more terse "Why would I be mad at you? Did you do something I should be mad at?" Those, too, were followed by reassurances that he would tell me if he were mad at me, though. A few years ago, he thought he'd come up with a perfect solution: "I will only be mad at you if you ask me why I'm mad at you."

He was not prepared for just how loopy my logic can get when it's under the influence of my anxieties. I said "Are you mad at me?" He said "Now I am." I asked why. He told me that I already knew. "Oh, is that it?" I replied in genuine relief. "I can live with that!"

I haven't been able to explain it any better to him than I'll explain it to you, but I'd rather risk his frustration over the question than resist asking it. His being mad about the question is a minor upset and, more importantly, a tangible one. I can deal with knowing he's mad at that specific thing. The unknown—and where my wretched mind runs with the possibilities—is unbearable. We've remained in this deadlock for years now.

There are also minor concerns that are simple enough to handle on their own but can sometimes build to bigger frustrations and ultimately manageable flare-ups. I can't always handle the sounds that come with living in close quarters with another human. When my resistance is low, I have a tendency to take his chewing, snoring, breathing and ankle cracking as more of a personal affront than a normal fact of life with an adult man who plays a bunch of rec hockey. In turn, he takes my wincing and occasional outbursts of exasperation as an attack on his being, not the frazzled responses of an autistic person who has been trying to ignore her sensory issues again, and is now upset by the sounds *and* her inability to contain her reaction to them.

The specifics of our problems might be unique to a half-autistic partnership, but I don't think the challenges or potential threats they pose to our mutual well-being are any worse than what I see functional non-autistic couples confronting. This isn't to minimize the issues that autistic people face when it comes to love, romance, sex and anything else you can throw into that enthralling and captivating aspect of the human experience. I don't necessarily believe that anyone is overestimating how hard healthy relationships can be for autistic people. I do think that we're underestimating how difficult it is for the rest of you, though.

As I've said, autistic people aren't always granted a level playing field when non-autistic people talk about the impact we have on their lives. It's a logical leap that you can see in the ways that self-branded "Autism Parents" or "Autism Warriors" discuss their afflicted kids. These small humans aren't compared to their real-life non-autistic counterparts; they're held against a romanticized ideal. Instead of addressing autism as one component of a multifaceted individual's life, they make autism the de facto explanation for everything they deem wrong with their child and assess their every struggle through that lens. From that limited perspective, everything, including the most basic annoying kid stuff—like stubbornness and pants aversion—becomes the dreaded Autism's fault.

The way that non-autistic people—and even some autistic people—talk about our romantic prospects or lack thereof appears to be based on the assumption that non-autistics are any better at these things. I've yet to see much proof of that. As far as I can tell, almost everyone sucks at dating and every permutation of what might come after that. No one really knows what they're doing. Because it's *hard*.[33]

Healthy sexual and/or romantic entanglements require the successful integration of two (or more, if you're all into that) lives, each with their own incredibly complicated mix of strengths, weaknesses, desires, needs, dreams, hopes, obstacles, circumstances and potential. You both have to meet the right person(s) at the right time in your lives. If you happen to win that lottery, you still have to work your asses off to make it work with each other, and within your lives, your families, your social circles, your work and the rest of the world. Even if you have all of the perfect raw material for a happy union, there's an entire genre of music—from Patty Smyth's "Sometimes Love Just Ain't Enough" to Van Halen's "Why Can't This Be Love"—dedicated to how that can fuck you up. Trying to navigate all of the above when you're also dealing with complex social issues isn't easy. But to treat autism as anything other than one piece of an overwhelmingly convoluted 3-D puzzle with no key is to do a massive disservice to every poor soul who attempts said puzzle.

It's also far from the sole hurdle facing an autistic individual in this realm. For example, you could argue that I, as an autistic person, am incredibly fortunate to have found a partner

....

33 To my non-autistic readers: I want to warn you that the next handful of paragraphs are going to be a shift in tone. I've been tempering my natural autistic inclination to spew large amounts of information in a single burst up until now in an effort to keep you as comfortable, engaged and amused as possible. But I fear that I need to be a bit of a lecturing eccentric aunt on these key points. So few autistics are given any kind of platform to tell our stories at all, and fewer still have a chance to touch on love and sex. Most of the material that non-autistic people have produced on the topic strikes me as patronization, mockery, exploitation or fear-mongering. I have a fairly rare chance to attempt to shift that conversation in my own small way here, and I believe that I owe it to my fellow autistics to squeeze as much as I can as seriously as I can into this section.
To my autistic readers: You'll be fine. It's info dump and mildly pedantic argument-making time!

who accepts me for who I am. To have an anchor in my life who is helpful and gentle with me when outside assistance might make a difference in whatever I'm going through, and patient and sympathetic when there's nothing anyone can do. Someone who takes care of all of the groceries because super-markets are an unlimited source of panic attacks for me, and has developed a spider sense for when I become overloaded in public, and knows how to extract us from situations before things get too out of control. And does all of the above without resentment or score-keeping. I won't disagree, but I think that I am equally if not more blessed to have found a male partner who accepts and supports me *as a female writer*. That's also a major part of my existence that requires a lot of understanding, patience and support, and one that many prospective partners wouldn't want to stick around for.

Autism isn't the sole cause of any strife in our relation-ships, either. It can absolutely be a factor in interpersonal conflicts, and in the way that we're able to handle them. Common vulnerable spots like emotional regulation and effective communication can become especially trying in periods of stress. This discord doesn't happen in a vacuum, though. The biggest ongoing source of disharmony in my parents' forty-year marriage involves task distribution. My father, who is also autistic, is worse at taking hints than I am. He would love nothing more than to be told, in detail and order, what needs to be done around the house. My mother, a woman born in the 1950s, has been conditioned to avoid dir-ect requests. There's always a part of her still convinced that issuing those kinds of directions is bossy, or nagging. They are both logically aware of this, but he can't always override his nature and she can't always fight her nurture. (As their autistic daughter, I've inherited both of their problems!)

Anyone who tries to tell you that autism alone has ruined their sex life or love life is either oversimplifying or scapegoating.

If you happen to lurk on the average autistic incel discussion online, you might start to notice that other personality issues might play a bigger role in cockblocking these charmers. For instance, some of them don't seem to appreciate that women are people. They're not wrong about the ways in which autistic people are devalued and misunderstood in our society, but their scope is far too limited. The actual problem isn't that autism prevents these mostly cisgender straight white men from getting laid like their non-autistic cishet white counterparts; it's that systemic ableism harms our lives on *all* fronts. Getting past first base isn't going to solve that.

Browse any first-hand accounts of the "Cassandra Phenomenon"—a.k.a. non-autistic people who believe that having an autistic or otherwise neurodivergent partner has left them affection-starved, burdened and traumatized—and you might recognize a similar pattern. These people are often trapped in toxic or unfulfilling relationships for many of the same reasons that people dating neurotypical assholes or unsuitable partners are. Not being able to express yourself smoothly, being a little clumsy with intimate interactions and needing a bit more space than the average human *isn't* really a choice for us. However, not giving a single fuck how those things might make other people feel and being completely uninterested in putting any effort toward a compromise that's healthy for you and your partner(s) *is* a choice. Failing to see your sexual or romantic partner as a complete person with their own value, needs and desires can be a comorbidity of autism, but it's not an inherent symptom in and of itself. It is a symptom of being a dick. So is refusing to have any compassion for what your partner might be going through and blaming them as the source of all of your problems.

My other concern with distilling the discussion about autism and love into a facile debate about whether or not we completely suck at it is that it fails to address other serious issues that we face. And it completely ignores a large percentage of us entirely. Anyone who wants to seriously—and productively—tackle this topic needs to acknowledge our entire spectrum, for lack of a better word, of genders and sexualities. We need to openly and honestly discuss what might help make us more fulfilled *and* safer.

As a cranky old(er) queer myself, I firmly believe that heteronormativity is a curse for everyone. It's a particularly harmful lens through which to discuss autism and love, though, because we are significantly queerer than non-autistic people. We are 7.59 times more likely to express gender variance, according to a 2014 study from the *Archives of Sexual Behavior*.[34] Further studies have reported similarly disproportionate rates. Seventy percent of us identify as non-heterosexual,[35] which is almost three times as un-straight as non-autistic people are. (Whether we are actually queerer than the normals or whether we're just more open to admitting it for a number of reasons is a topic of much speculation among my fellow LGBTQ autistics, but that's a whole other dialogue.) It's also important to note that this 70 percent includes asexual people, and it's absolutely vital to stress that asexuality is valid. I fear that, in some of our efforts to push back against the old stereotype that all autistic people are sexless beings, allosexual autistic people ended up erasing and hurting our asexual counterparts. We come in every gender. Some of us have no gender. Our interests in sex and who we might be interested in having it with—or not—are as individual as we are. Any conversations about autism and

34   J.F Strang et al., "Increased Gender Variance in Autism Spectrum Disorders and Attention Deficit Hyperactivity Disorder," *Archives of Sexual Behavior* (2014) 43(8): 1525–33. See https://doi.org/10.1007/s10508-014-0285-3.
35   C.E.S Rudolph et al., "Brief Report: Sexual Orientation in Individuals with Autistic Traits: Population Based Study of 47,000 Adults in Stockholm County," *Journal of Autism and Developmental Disorders* (2018) 48(2): 619–24. See https://www.ncbi.nlm.nih.gov/pubmed/29086210.

love that don't at least try to address this fact are going to be about as effective as a seventeen-year-old film dork trying to score at the pool hall with Cronenberg quotes.

We must also be careful, balanced and respectful when we're talking about the issue of sex and safety. Autistic people can and do have healthy sex lives and any pearl-clutching attempt to view our sexuality only in terms of how it can be exploited by predators is going to do as much harm as good. Autistic adolescents—hell, autistics of all ages—do need to be encouraged to establish boundaries, and to express and recognize consent. Teaching these without explicitly acknowledging that it's perfectly normal to feel desire and to consensually act on it can lead to some issues of its own, though. We cannot underestimate or downplay the threat of sexual assault—especially not when autistic girls and women are almost three times as likely to have experienced sexual abuse as our non-autistic counterparts[36]—but this cannot be the entire focus of autistic sexual education. Yet education alone can't help us if no one stands up to address how society's ableism makes disabled people such easy and convenient targets for predators. (And if non-autistic people truly care about protecting us from sexual abuse and assault, then they're going to have to do some real soul-searching about the ways behavioural therapies and social conditioning can erode our autonomy.)

This is obviously too much to try to insert into a casual chat with a stranger who is trying to imagine wider potentials for their child than the outside world may have given them so far. It strains the seams of a personal essay. But I do try, in whatever way is appropriate, to widen their hopes and

....

36   V. Ohlsson Gotby et al., "Childhood Neurodevelopmental Disorders and Risk of Coercive Sexual Victimization in Childhood and Adolescence: A Population-Based Prospective Twin Study," *Journal of Child Psychology and Psychiatry* (2018) 59(9): 957–65. See https://www.ncbi.nlm.nih.gov/pubmed/29570782.

refocus their fears. My experiences may have left me with little to offer in conversations about love and lust among the neurodivergent, but they've also left me aware of how little valuable information on the topic exists at all.

Reflecting on my naivety and cluelessness absolutely makes me appreciate the need for better education for autistic people—and better awareness for everyone—when it comes to issues of consent and safety. Knowing how horny I was[37] makes me appreciate the necessity of respecting our desires and fostering an environment where they can develop as healthily and safely as possible. Remembering how gay and isolated I was fuels my need to make sure everyone's included.

As for my marriage, well, that makes me think and want a lot of things. I don't mind anyone looking at where I am now in life as a positive outcome. It is. But I'd prefer it to be for the right reasons. Instead of looking to me as proof that their child might not be alone or unloved in life, I want people to think of me as a sign that their child might find what they are seeking in life. I don't want my case adding to anyone else's expectations for that child. Being lonely and frustrated sucks enough for its own reasons, and there's no need exacerbate that feeling with the worry that you're not assuaging your parents' anxieties about your prospects after they're gone. Or with the knowledge that what you want for yourself isn't in line with what comforts them. I don't even want my example to reinforce any standards that hold romantic or sexual love above all others. Being able to bang my favourite person and enjoy a few tax breaks because we signed some papers and had a party once are cool benefits and all, but I don't think our relationship would be any less important or valid if those things weren't on the table.

....

37 And continue to be. I'm basically a live-action adult version of the butt-obsessed, erotic friend fiction–writing Tina Belcher from *Bob's Burgers*.

If anyone wants to treat my happy union as some kind of extraordinary result, then let's be clear about why it is actually a miracle, too. If there's one thing I've learned as I've bumbled through my love life and lent a supportive ear to so many friends, both neurotypical and neurodivergent, it's that love and sex make almost no sense at all. The fact that I've somehow managed, through no fault on their parts or merit on my own, to be more successful than some of them just goes to show what a crapshoot it all is. No one knows what they're doing. Can having a condition that affects social interactions make these things more difficult? Yes, but not exponentially so. I've talked enough non-autistic friends through communication breakdowns and helped them hyper-analyze enough vague hints from prospective partners to know that everyone struggles. It's actually astounding that we're not all bleeding and sobbing and listening to problematic British blowhards we should have cancelled years ago[38] all the time. It's incredible that *anyone* finds who and what they want in life—and that it works out in any way.

The other side of it, though, is that if no one knows what they're doing, then it stands to reason that everyone *could* have a chance. If I, a dorky, awkward, half-cynical/half-earnest hybrid seeking same, can stumble into a modicum of happiness in this wretched world, perhaps others can too. If I can tell you a love story—as riddled with casual asides about poop and Sammy Hagar–fronted power ballads[39] as it is— then maybe, just maybe, anything is possible.

....
38 Fucking Morrissey.
39 "Why Can't This Be Love," which Aaron would argue also counts as poop. And which I referenced in this essay mostly to exasperate him.

STEP SEVEN

Find a healthy outlet for your identity crisis. Like professional pillow fighting

AT TWO POINTS IN MY LIFE I VERY DELIBERATELY DECIDED TO change my personality for a specific purpose. When I wanted to be liked, or at least left alone, I patterned myself after anyone and everyone who seemed remotely lovable. When I wanted to be hated, I turned to an equally obvious template: myself.

I tried the first one for the same reason that I did most things between the ages of nine and fourteen. I was bullied, terrified, desperate to do anything to alleviate that onslaught ... and not exactly filled with any healthier or more mature ideas because I was spending my formative years being bullied and terrified. I did the second one for the same reason that I've made a disconcerting number of impetuous choices over the course of my ostensibly mature adult life: because I fell in love with professional wrestling.

I started following wrestling early in my relationship with Aaron. I was a raging snob who had grown up on art house films and classic literature and was viciously baffled to discover that this man I adored, who was smart and otherwise seemed to have good taste, could be so taken with it. So I watched some programming from what was then the

WWF out of a perverse curiosity. What could he see in this bread and circus I had always dismissed as lowest common denominator trash? Within a week, I sure got it.

Once I opened my mind to it, wrestling immediately appealed to me as someone who loves narrative in any medium. It was potent and vital, witty and melodramatic, with a powerful, almost fourth wall and boundary-breaking connection to its audience that no other contemporary art form was even attempting. I didn't just love it as a fan—I was completely enraptured with it as a baby writer who wanted to figure out how to recreate that magic with her own storytelling. (And it continues to be a wonderful and bizarre influence on me. One of the essays in this book was inspired by the brilliantly bonkers narrative structure of a match from a Japanese promotion called DDT[40] Pro-Wrestling. The title of which was, roughly translated, "Captain's Fall Anal Explosion Time Difference Web News Posting Tag Death Match.")

As my casual interest grew into an autistically obsessive deep dive into the world of pro wrestling, I started to daydream about what kind of wrestler I'd be. There was no question that I wanted to be a heel. As a fan, I simply thought the bad guys were more interesting than their often one-dimensional do-gooder baby face counterparts. As a writer, I was thoroughly intrigued by the complex blend of physical and verbal storytelling that went into crafting the antagonistic characters and their stories, and wanted to try it for myself. As a former bullied kid, I found the idea of being hated on purpose kind of refreshing and maybe even liberating. How nice it would be to make my off-putting nature useful for once.

As for a gimmick, I went with the most villainous thing I knew: a weird, overcompensating smart girl with a chip on

....
40 Dramatic Dream Team.

her shoulder. I called this monster Sarah Bellum, because how could any nerd named Sarah resist the pun? In my spare time, I'd dream up snide and condescending promos for her—and delivered a few of them when I was home alone.

A few years into my fixation, a fellow *Chart* writer and host of a local wrestling and MMA radio show told me that he was working for a new sports entertainment promotion called the Pillow Fight League. The fights themselves would be "real." The outcomes wouldn't be predetermined and any move from MMA, boxing or amateur wrestling would be legal as long as it employed a pillow at the point of contact. The characters, storylines and overall spectacle would absolutely be taking their cues from pro wrestling, though. They were looking for fighters and he thought I'd be perfect for it.

Sarah Bellum, the scholar of pillow fighting, became a reality.

Autistic people love pro wrestling.

This is a completely unscientific observation made by an admittedly biased observer. But in my experience as an autistic wrestling fan who has spent a lot of time interacting with other autistic people and comparing notes about our lives, I've noticed that a disproportionate number of us seem to have an intense interest in this universe.[41]

I have three theories about this phenomenon.

....

41 I'd love to offer you some more concrete evidence of this phenomenon than my own interactions with other autistic people, but that's all I'm working with here. The "experts" spend most of their time researching and reporting on the possible causes and cures of autism. Occasionally they try to figure out why we don't like making eye contact and how to teach/force us to make eye contact. Autistic people are left to piece together a basic understanding of every other aspect of our existence through anecdata.

Part of me has wondered if the disparity between autistic people and non-autistic people in this regard is less a matter of taste than a matter of openness. Wrestling is a brilliant art form filled with limitless potential for sweeping, operatic plots and stunningly intimate character studies. Sure, it can also be overwrought, self-indulgent, offensive, aimlessly provocative or just plain shit, but that potential exists in all media. Some of my favourite art films are aimlessly provocative shit. The percentage of non-autistic people who would be willing to admit their interest to the world—or to themselves—would probably be similar to the percentage of autistic people if wrestling wasn't derided as being lowbrow and low class. The stigma that still surrounds the medium is far less of a concern for autistics. We're either unable to pick up on the subtle social cues that tell us that loving wrestling is improper or uncool, or simply don't care because we're already such misunderstood misfits in so many other aspects of our lives.

Or maybe it's just that, for those of us who use entertainment to help us try to understand and interact with the non-autistic world around us, wrestling's broad themes and theatrically exaggerated expressions offer accessible (if not entirely healthy) insights into everything from betrayal and social machinations to teamwork, friendship and overcoming challenges.

I've recently come up with a third theory, though. While many still dismiss wrestling because it's "fake," it might be wrestling's blurred and ever-shifting line between fiction and reality, particularly when it comes to the relationship between wrestlers and their characters, that appeals to us most of all. Some wrestlers play entirely fictional supernatural beings. Others inhabit barely exaggerated versions of themselves. How much of their own life creeps into their performance is unique to each individual and not always obvious to others. For those of us who mask, a fairly common autistic behaviour that involves consciously and subconsciously hiding our noticeable autistic traits in an effort to appear more socially acceptable, what could be more relatable—what could be more real—than this constant navigation between person and persona?

I wasn't thinking about any of this when I joined the PFL. I didn't know for certain that I was autistic yet, much less what that actually entailed. I strongly suspected it was the case, though. When a friend had suggested I look up the symptoms for Asperger's syndrome and "high-functioning autism" in my early twenties, I checked almost all of the boxes. But I didn't really know what to do with the information, because there were no meaningful options for testing or treatment for adults in Ontario who couldn't afford private services. So I just tucked that suspicion in the back of my mind, and gave myself a little credit for fixing any and all problems I might have had with social skills, self-regulation, etc. And proceeded to craft an elaborate alter ego for my professional pillow fighting career that would finally bury any lingering pain and resentment I still had from the bad years. As any normal person would.

I thought Sarah Bellum was going to be an exorcism of sorts, a way to make use of and possibly make peace with my less than idyllic self during my less than idyllic formative years. Someone I could inhabit for fun because her failings were no longer my own. I was kind of tolerable now. I could (sort of) make friends. I was well on my way to being a legitimate jock! I wasn't that weird little charmless nerd anymore. I would just play her on the martial arts mats and on the mic.

"You're not a heel," Aaron insisted when I first started sharing my plans for my character with him. "No one is going to boo you. You're so much smaller than the other women. No matter how much shit you talk, you'll still be the underdog."

He was right about the size differential. If the PFL had weight classes, I would have been at least two below all but one of my fellow fighters. My height and reach also put me at a disadvantage. The poor lovestruck fool was sorely misguided about the rest, though.

"You didn't know me when I was younger," I replied, which was fair. "You have no idea." Which was not. *I like you and therefore have cause to believe that others might, too* being a valid argument.

I approached Sarah Bellum's realization with a conviction and self-assurance absent in almost every other area of my life. My social interactions were uniformly riddled with self-doubt and anxiety, and I second-guessed my every breath for weeks afterwards. I was so insecure about my work as a young writer that my process had become almost comically self-flagellating, even by typical self-loathing writer standards. But I *knew* that I could obliterate any potential goodwill the audience might feel compelled to extend to me within thirty seconds of opening my mouth. I'd been putting people off inadvertently for my whole life.

I flattened my vocal range back into a few nasal notes. I dropped the exaggerated smiles and raised eyebrows that I'd been affecting in an effort to portray kindness and interest after years of being told that people couldn't read my face. I stopped trying to hide that strange, flimsy cockiness that brutally unpopular kids sometimes have. The one we develop to try to convince ourselves and everyone else that people only hate us because we're so brilliant, and they're just jealous. I pulled my hair into a prissy bun and my mouth into a tight smirk. I wore my own glasses. With a stiff posture and even stiffer, overly formal speech, I demanded quiet and declared my love of rules.

I earned my first boos two lines into my promo at our first live event. In retrospect, I must have been overwhelmed. Every aspect of the show was a sensory nightmare. The jeers and screams of a couple of hundred bloodthirsty people were bouncing off the walls of a small, dank goth club. It was hot and typically Toronto humid and we were all soaked in our own sweat, each other's, and whatever was stuck to the disturbingly under-sterilized mats. But all I remember was the satisfaction I felt.

For a brief, magically suspect moment in time, the PFL started to take off. Our first shows, held at a dying Toronto goth bar that had *Doctor Who* fetish gear tucked into its basement for some reason, sold out quickly. We started touring and held successful events in Windsor, Montreal and New York. International media attention and an ultimately failed TV deal followed. As I'd demonstrated an (over) enthusiasm for talking, I was trusted with a large portion of the promotional duties. In addition to our shows, I had the opportunity to hone my character on TV, radio and a segment of VH1's *Celebrity Fit Club* where I rolled around a La Jolla tae kwon do studio with a pyjama-clad Maureen McCormick.[42]

Being Sarah Bellum was easy. In many cases, it was more comfortable than being Sarah Kurchak was. I seamlessly slipped into her tics and mannerisms for events and interviews. It took nothing to adopt her quips and self-possession ... and her bountiful character flaws. I told myself that this was merely the mark of a good performer. That the reason I felt more at ease being her in front of hundreds of bloodthirsty fans or live in a Times Square storefront studio than

....

42   Best known for playing Marcia Brady on the original *Brady Bunch* sitcom (1969–1974 on ABC), McCormick also appeared on the fifth season of *Fit Club* in 2007. She was lovely, but I'm a lifelong Jan type. Fighting the actual Marcia, Marcia, Marcia dredged up some interesting emotions.

I did when I was being myself in a casual one-on-one conversation was because I was just such a natural.

This was, I slowly came to realize, not entirely the case. I did seem to have some skill in that arena—and all of the hours I'd spent obsessively studying VHS tapes of The Rock and Chris Jericho's promos had clearly paid off. But I was vastly overestimating how much of my time in the PFL was a performance, and how much was semi-consciously working through complex issues of identity, self-concept and self-acceptance by insulting and beating up my friends on television and in crowded bars across Ontario and New York State.

When I became a part of the *Chart* magazine microcosm, I felt like I was less alone in the universe, and like I'd finally found some piece of my place in it. I got to work on something I really cared about with other like-minded people who felt the same way about the same things. Including each other. Joining the PFL was like my *Chart* experience hopped up on some cocktail of performance-enhancing drugs, hallucinogens and cat memes. One of my best friends, the artist formerly known as Betty Clock'er, originally joined because she was under the impression that the PFL would be something between a fight club and informal group therapy. We'd hit each other with pillows for an hour, cry and then hug it out. She may have misread the audition call, but she wasn't exactly wrong, either.

If you're the type of person who signs up for something as unapologetically absurd and niche as a professional pillow fighting league, there is a strong chance that you'll find at least some sort of kinship with the other ne'er-do-wells who think that's a good idea. With a few dramatic exceptions, I did. Whether we were writers, alt fashion models, chefs, students, a waitress unbiting her tongue for the first time in twenty years, a "drug analyst" (that's what she wrote on her application) or some combination of the above, we found some unique and thrilling common ground.

These bonds only intensified as we banded together against increasingly bizarre circumstances and erratic management. (GLOW, Netflix's fictionalized account of the bonkers eighties promotion Gorgeous Ladies of Wrestling, is an alarmingly accurate portrait of how I spent/wasted my mid-twenties.) The women of the PFL became my found family and my war buddies. We'd yell at each other in character and genuinely try to beat the snot out of each other to the best of our limited abilities in front of the crowds and cameras. Backstage, we'd giggle, cry, hug, trade increasingly dirty in-jokes, talk about how much we loved each other and try to make some sense of whatever the fuck was happening to our lives.

Somewhere between this maladjusted but largely loving embrace of my reprobate sisterhood and that strange liminal space between fiction and reality that the PFL borrowed from wrestling, I started to work on some stuff. I wasn't aware of it at the time, but I think this implausible environment finally gave me the breathing room to figure out who and what I could be in a way that the high stakes of "normal" childhood and adolescent socialization had never allowed.

The word "reclaim" feels so corny to me in a context like this, but being Sarah Bellum did allow me to revisit some parts of myself that I'd assumed had to be discarded entirely. Turning them into some muddy hybrid of an entirely separated character and an exaggerated persona meant that I could see if that version of myself had always been as unwanted as I'd assumed without risking too much in other aspects of my life. Playing around with her foibles allowed me to test out a version of myself that I wasn't quite ready to *be* anywhere else yet. If Sarah Bellum did something that rubbed people the wrong way, I could say that was the character. If she did something that they didn't hate, though, well

... that action and reaction could be stored away for Sarah Kurchak's future use.

This sort of hiding in plain sight as your true self, or playing a character who is actually playing some part of your life that's been kept secret for whatever reason, can definitely be used in bad faith. I'd be lying if I said that I never gave in to the impulse to write off an actual human mistake as something I'd done on purpose as Bellum. (And I've winced in recognition when I've caught some of my favourite wrestlers pulling similar shit.) If you're not just using it as a way to shirk accountability, though, this type of public performance provides a unique opportunity for anyone who has, out of necessity, been forced to hide themselves. In "character," you can comfortably test the waters and see if it's safe to stop.

At some point, Bellum ceased getting quite so many boos. In part, this was because I was a terrible fighter and, with a few notable exceptions, was routinely humiliated in matches. After a while, booing the shitty little one who kept valiantly getting her ass kicked by her bigger and more talented opponents just felt mean. Pity wasn't the only reason for the shift, though. It also turned out that Ms. Bellum wasn't entirely loathsome after all. Eventually, she evolved from a pompous heel into an occasionally sympathetic tweener. She had a chip on her shoulder and an overconfidence in her brain that was probably the result of some deep-seated insecurities as a person, but she was trying her best in her own clumsy way. She consistently said the wrong things, but sometimes she was funny. She had an ugly competitive streak, but loved her fellow pillow-fighting misfits as much as she hated losing to them. A bit of a mess—and a bit of a dick as a result—but not without her charms. She was, in fact, the person who Aaron had seen all along, and one who the other women of the PFL embraced as one of their own. She was someone I liked *being*.

(To give you an idea of just how well my PFL family got me, let me tell you about the first time I ran into our ref, Matt, after my diagnosis. "I was amazed when I heard that," Matty said to me.

My heart sank. While most of the people who had known me as a child—especially my old teachers—received the news of my Official Autism with a complete absence of surprise, people who had met me in adulthood were almost uniformly incredulous. And it hurt to see a big part of myself, one that had seemed at least somewhat obvious to me the whole time, questioned by people I thought understood me.

Once again, I dejectedly assembled all of my talking points in my head about what I'd been like as a kid, how I'd learned to hide this or that, and how the stereotypes about autism aren't really in line with its reality, and started to run through them for him.

"No," he stopped me. "I meant that I was surprised you hadn't been diagnosed ages ago."

I almost cried in relief as he started listing all of the reasons that he knew.)

The PFL eventually fell apart, both because of management issues and because it was a professional pillow fighting league and what else was it going to do, really? But I've held on to the friendships I made and the shit I figured out there. Of all of the silly and inconsequential things I've done in my life, this was easily the silliest and most inconsequential, and yet it was the source of something bordering on catharsis. Finally being diagnosed with autism helped me to make some sense out of a lot of aspects of my life. The subsequent years of autism-friendly therapy that I've undergone have allowed me to work on a lot of issues from a more informed perspective. And yet nothing I've actively done to try to make my life as an autistic person better or more bearable has been quite as effective as the two years I spent being two people and hammering out the first hints of an actual sense of self in the secret protected space between them.

As much as I still grumble about certain parts of the PFL now—and as much as I try to laugh off the growing nostalgia I have for that period of my life, lest I sound like even more of a sad old lady clinging to her glory years than I am—I remain confused but grateful for all of it. And for the women who still call me Bellum.

STEP EIGHT

Drink

I WAS STRAIGHT EDGE—NO DRINKING, NO SMOKING, NO DRUGS—until I was almost twenty. This was less of an ideological choice than I liked to claim it was at the time.

My ties to the culture were suspect at best. I didn't hang out with other straight edge people or go out to any of their shows. I didn't try to join any servers or message boards related to straight edge culture—although I lurked for a while. Its music wasn't my thing, and its stance on caffeine and sex were even less appealing.

My exposure to alcohol and drugs was even more limited and more disagreeable, though. My parents never touched the stuff. They weren't strict or even outwardly disapproving, it just wasn't their thing. They both somehow came of age in the seventies without so much as a toke between them. My dad stopped what little casual drinking he had been doing when he had an allergic reaction to beer at the CNE and almost died in the middle of the fairgrounds. Mom lost interest in drinking when she started dating him. (A teenage misadventure involving the Rex Hotel in Welland, cigarette paper art and an aborted game of drunk hockey that Mom did her best to turn into a cautionary tale may have played a role as well.)

The only time I saw any alcohol consumption when I was growing up was at family events where my uncles would take over the TV, down a bunch of beer, yell at whatever sports happened to be on and swiftly overwhelm my delicate senses. I could smell the beer from the next room, and it made me gag. Their yelling made my chest tighten. I couldn't stand to be around any of it. Other kids my age started experimenting with that stuff well after they stopped talking to me, so I was never around them imbibing, either.

So straight edge was less of an ethos than an image rehabilitation project for me. My strong hypochondriac streak had me half-convinced that I'd magically inherited a fatal beer allergy. I was scared of my uncles. And I faced no peer pressure because I had no peers. Drawing Xs on my hands and pretending to be a badass with an ethos made me feel marginally better about myself.

With more exposure to the outside world in my late teens came more exposure to booze and booze culture, and it really wasn't like anything that I'd imagined it to be. Sure, I met some boorish drunks and witnessed a fair number of ill-advised decisions and yes, I started to recognize the signs of something—or someone—not being fun anymore. But it wasn't the all-encompassing den of sin, decay and misery that I'd been expecting. Or at least it wasn't any more seething a pit of those things than any other culture or pastime I'd witnessed thus far in my life. And unlike almost any other things that a vast majority of people seemed to appreciate, I didn't hate it.

I smelled types of alcohol that didn't propel me into a full-body gag, and met people who enjoyed it without yelling at TVs in a way that propelled me into a full-body wince. Over time, I was offered a substantial amount of proof that not every sip ends in near death or brain injury. I witnessed plenty of misadventure, but the majority of it was benign.

With a touch of peer encouragement—it was far too polite, tentative and dotted with assurances that I could stop at any time if I was uncomfortable or otherwise unpleased to call it *pressure*—I decided to try a few things out.

My first experiment, at a Christmas party hosted by *Chart*'s publishers, was a perversely heartwarming failure. I sipped at a number of mixed drinks lovingly crafted for me by a colleague[43] who was enthusiastic about helping to introduce me to the world of cocktails. And maybe even more enthusiastic about raiding her underpaying bosses' liquor cabinet in support of the cause. But nothing clicked. I lost interest again for a while. One night early in our relationship, Aaron took me to a sports bar in his neighbourhood ... and I ordered ice cream.

A year later, I got it into my head to try coolers at the Legion and a whole new and possibly questionable world opened up to me. With the aid of two bottles of sickly sweet Smirnoff Ice (I know, I was twenty), I had fun in public! Sure, the already too-bright lights seemed to get brighter as they got a bit fuzzier, but the background noise dulled into a more amiable blur and I spent hours participating in a group conversation without spending the entire time worrying about what I was doing wrong! That shit was like magic juice.

I started to drink—and continue to drink—because I enjoy the beverages themselves and the activities that surround them. I appreciate an elaborately presented cocktail at a tiki bar, a pint of cider (beer remains vile and gag-inducing) at a moderately quiet pub, or whatever is free at the open bar industry events I occasionally scrounge up enough clout to get invited to and guts to attend. The flavour and the texture of prosecco are appealing to me, as is the act of splitting a

....
43 Who wishes to remain nameless in this story, even though it's pretty innocent and she remains a beloved friend, accomplice and source of good booze to this day.

bottle of it with a friend at a low-key house party, or during an afternoon of binging spy shows from the 1960s. I keep a detailed list, broken down by casino and ranked by preference, of my favourite drinks to order in Las Vegas while I'm playing and yelling at simulated horse racing games.

But I'd be lying if I said that I didn't also appreciate booze's use as a social aid, a confidence booster and a method of self-medication. Or that I have never leaned on it a bit too much during times of great stress, or even more severe than usual awkwardness.

Here's a random example of my alcohol-infused social skill building in action, from the last time I had a drink: I went to a wrestling show alone and met up with an old colleague and his friend. They were amiable and chatty, but I was me. Then I ordered a cider.

In addition to the crisp, refreshing taste of apples, the drink gave me something concrete and sensible to do with my hands. Immediately, that removed one layer of stress. Holding the can meant that I didn't have to worry about making weird gestures or movements, and could focus more on our conversation. When that conversation hit a natural pause that I wasn't sure how to navigate, I took a sip. This essential part of the drinking process didn't just deliver more cider into my body, it allowed me to cover any panic I felt over not knowing what to say next, and allowed me a brief moment to regroup before I tried again. After a few more sips, I became less hyper-aware and hyper-critical of my mannerisms and cadence. Which led to me unironically declaring myself "the Royce Gracie of pillow fighting,"[44] but nobody's perfect and at least I was among friends who knew what that meant.

....

44 Because, like the breakthrough stars of the early Ultimate Fighting Championship shows, I had to use leverage against my much larger opponents in the PFL. These are the kinds of conversations you can successfully have at a wrestling matinee on a weekday.

Alcohol dulls the stage parent–esque voice that is always screaming in the back of my mind, monitoring and criticizing my every breath, taunting me to do better and reminding me that I'm probably screwing things up miserably. In the presence of fellow weirdos, this allows me to further relax and just enjoy the company of people who never expected nor wanted any smoother or more becoming behaviour out of me. In the presence of normals and strangers, it at least makes me care a bit less if I do fuck it all up. Which, for me, can be the difference between hiding silently in the corner all night and giving the whole talking-to-other-people thing a shot. It's clearly not the best or the healthiest coping mechanism, but for someone with my kind of life and my kind of work with my kind of brain, it's sometimes the only feasible one.

Like most things related to autistic adult life, there is very little research that's been done on the potential relationship between substance use, abuse and addiction and our neurology. Part of the reason is that most people fail to acknowledge our existence at all. Research, services, funding and awareness campaigns are largely focused on children, with little consideration for the fact that those children will grow up and still be autistic. Even when we are considered, though, misconceptions about what autism is and who autistic people are can leave a lot of pressing concerns unexamined.

"Until recently, researchers held that addiction among people with autism is rare, although there wasn't much solid evidence for this view," Maia Szalavitz wrote in a feature on autism and addiction for *Spectrum* in 2017.[45] "It seemed plausible, though: Many people with autism have a penchant for strictly following rules, which would seem to make them

....
45 Maia Szalavitz, "The Hidden Link Between Autism and Addiction," *Spectrum*, for *The Atlantic* (March 2, 2017). See https://www.theatlantic.com/health/archive/2017/03/autism-and-addiction/518289/.

less likely to try alcohol or illegal drugs. Because people with autism are often isolated from their peers, this could protect them from the peer pressure that can lead to youthful experimentation. And many people diagnosed with autism decades ago had severe features; a person who can't live independently has few opportunities to become addicted."

Researchers who have pushed past these preconceptions are starting to piece together a much different story. According to the findings of one Swedish study published in the *Journal of Autism and Developmental Disorders* in 2017,[46] autistic people with an IQ of one hundred or higher could be at twice the risk of developing an addiction to alcohol and drugs as non-autistic people are. This risk is significantly increased for those with co-occurring ADHD. The results may have come as a shock to the uninitiated, but autistic people and those who work with us on such issues are somewhat less surprised.

"I work with a lot of people with [autism] who have all kinds of impulsive behaviours," Eric Hollander, director of the Autism and Obsessive Compulsive Spectrum Program at Albert Einstein College of Medicine in New York told *Spectrum*. "In fact, that's one of the main targets when people come in for treatment. Either they're out of control in terms of shopping on the internet or gaming, or they're just addicted to the internet."

There are a number of scientific theories for why and how autistic people are potentially more likely to develop addictions than the non-autistic population. Impulsivity and repetitive and compulsive behaviours all occupy the middle of that Venn diagram. There are possible genetic and

....
46   A. Butwicka et al., "Increased Risk for Substance Use-Related Problems in Autism Spectrum Disorders: A Population-Based Cohort Study." *Journal of Autism and Developmental Disorders* (2017) 47(1): 80–89. See https://doi.org/10.1007/s10803-016-2914-2.

neurochemical connections between the autism and addiction. But there also seems to be a strong social component to why we take up addictive substances and behaviours at all. Most of the autistic people with first-hand experience with addiction who were interviewed for the *Spectrum* article started drinking and taking drugs for many of the same reasons I did.

I don't have a drug or alcohol addiction. This is less about willpower or lack of genetic predisposition on my part than it is a difference in vices (Hollander's internet observation hits far too close to home). I wouldn't go so far as to call my use of alcohol—which, outside of vacations and film festival season, averages a few glasses a week—a problem, either. I am aware that it is one of many makeshift coping mechanisms that I employ to help get me through life, though. And I am aware that my use of it as such has not always been entirely healthy or wise.

Using alcohol as a social performance enhancing drug is, at best, a precarious choice. Beyond the obvious risk for abuse and addiction, finding the right dose is a most delicate science. The right amount takes the edge off and allows me to try to engage more like a normal person, without the full weight of all my past failures and anxious internal analysis suffocating my efforts. Too much, though, and alcohol starts telling me that I can make normal people like me *for myself* the way it tells normal people that they're actually really good at dancing or singing. With similar results.

My natural body language (which ranges from accidentally insular to accidentally flirtatious), imperfect volume gauge, mile-a-minute hyper-verbal chatter and intense, narrow focus can be a lot for the uninitiated. And I feel a strange compulsion to talk about *Dead Souls*, the novel by Russian/Ukrainian dramatist Nikolai Gogol, when I've had a few. I am largely fine with who I am these days, but there are portions of my personality and general being that aren't really fit for mainstream consumption and it's better when I'm at least alert or sober enough in public to keep a lid on them.

At the right level of drunk, I almost inevitably become convinced that I've been overreacting and that I should just relax, because people will like me! This prompts me to earnestly approach strangers and mild acquaintances with all of the enthusiasm and appeal of a pound puppy furiously wagging a poop-sodden tail around, expecting everyone to love it like the other dogs. (This description, inspired by a true story about my first dog's adoption, was written sober and with great consideration. So you can extrapolate how the actual tipsy freeform interactions go.)

It can be true. There really is someone for everyone and you can find your people when you have the courage, liquid or otherwise, to be yourself. Some velvet morning a few years ago, I awoke to find a Facebook request from one of Aaron's hockey friends. I remembered meeting him at a league party the night before, and that we'd excitedly bonded over some topic, but I couldn't recall the details. So I asked Aaron.

"Yeah ... you two were talking about Russian literature all night," he said with what I choose to interpret as a mix of exhaustion and fondness.

With this reminder and more fully regained consciousness, I was able to piece together our night. My new best friend had mentioned, in passing, that he was in the middle of reading the aforementioned *Dead Souls*. I squealed, "It's *funny*, right?!" And we spent ages giddily discussing this surprisingly wry book that we'd both picked up because we liked depressing Russian writers like Dostoevsky. And because we thought it might have something to do with the Joy Division song of the same name.

Artisanal cocktails (and sleep deprivation) at a film festival party once inspired me to insert myself into a stranger's conversation about Gaspar Noé's *Love* to deliver this gem: "Didn't you think the ejaculation scene bore an aesthetic resemblance to Tammy's 'I Ain't Gonna Spread for No Roses' music video from *Kids in the Hall*?"[47] We meet up whenever he's in town.

My tipsy unadulterated Kurchak moments aren't usually reciprocated or received so well, though. The hit my cognitive processing takes with any degree of inebriation also hampers the vigilant watch I try to keep on other people's responses. Which means I can't even notice that people are politely trying to excuse themselves until it's too late. At another Christmas party for another Canadian music publication many years later, a pair of vodka and Cokes on an empty stomach assured me that I was among like-minded people who would probably like me and I should totally go for it. So I spent the whole night wandering around, initiating conversations, saying things that I thought were funny out loud and tossing the occasional "We should hang out!" into the mix until one of the full-time staff members took me aside to show me their fancy coffee machine and make me coffee. It took me a couple of days to figure out that none of those plans I tried to make were going to come to fruition and a week to realize the coffee was likely an attempt to sober me up. I still wonder what other hints I missed that night.

Using alcohol or other substances as self-medication is an even trickier line to walk. I think alcohol can help to dull my senses, which can make management of some sensory concerns temporarily easier. I strongly suspect that all of those outlandish cocktails I love so much when I'm in Las Vegas are part of the reason why I can mostly handle

....

47   Yes, this is really how I talk when left to my own devices. No, it's not entirely lost on me why some people might not like me. In my defence, the money shot from Noé's 2015 X-rated 3-D art film bears a striking resemblance to the jizzing roses from the *KITH* skit.

the city's constant *Wheel of Fortune* chimes, flashing lights, smoke, carpet-bombed air freshener and ceaseless flow of uninhibited humanity.

I'm not much of drug person at all (my opinion of them is similar to Dorothy Parker's eschewal of suicide in her poem "Resumé": all of the methods of delivery suck, so why bother?) but the first time I tried pot, deep into my twenties, felt like a minor revelation. It was like I could feel my brain slow down. All of the tension, the panic, the eleventeen different tangents and the looped soundtrack of self-criticism eased and one single train of thought emerged. I spent the rest of the day repeatedly watching the episode of the *Backyardigans* where they pretend to be pirates and asking Aaron if "this is how it feels in normal people's heads all the time."

There's a tipping point where the opposite becomes true for me, though. Too much alcohol and light feels piercings and sound can feel like cudgel hitting my body. In addition to the general misery they cause, hangovers—and even mild dehydration—are becoming increasingly overwhelming sensory experiences for me as I get older. I spent the first hangover of my thirties trembling and cold sweating in bed, frantically googling phrases like "hangovers different in thirties," "hangover symptoms death" and "hangover when to go to hospital" on my phone until the screen's already low brightness setting starting causing more distress than all of my death-mimicking symptoms combined. More than a nibble of edibles makes me dizzy and triggers panic attacks. I discovered this side effect after trying to self-medicate my way through a vicious bout of deadline-induced stress and spending the rest of the night on the floor with a kettle bell on my chest (in my panic, it seemed like a good weighted blanket substitute) muttering about the tragic irony of getting an anxiety attack for trying to prevent an anxiety attack.

And then there's, you know, the whole part where indulging in potentially addictive substances and/or behaviours in an effort to self-medicate can have unfortunate or even serious consequences.

I'm heartened by the fact that the autistic people interviewed in the *Spectrum* article were able to work on their addictions and move on to coping mechanisms that were healthier and more effective once they were finally diagnosed with autism. But I still worry that any research and treatment related to autism and addiction that doesn't at least acknowledge the lack of better resources available for autistic adults won't be going deep or far enough. Self-knowledge alone has helped me in a lot of ways, but it hasn't been a complete game changer. Finally getting diagnosed did give me a new perspective on many facets of my life, and helped me to reconsider my approaches to many of them. It maybe even nudged me toward maybe forgiving myself for some of my foibles and mistakes. It didn't significantly alter my drinking or my approach to it, though. At most, I developed a better understanding of why I appreciated it and then kept on doing it.

About a year after I was diagnosed, I went to an industry happy hour while covering the Toronto International Film Festival for *Chart*. I didn't know anyone there, so I grabbed a glass of free wine and skulked around the outskirts of the venue. Another wine and a good five laps later, a publicist took pity on the weird woman orbiting the event and took me under her wing. At some point during our chat, I mentioned that I was autistic. She expressed surprise. "Well," I said, gesturing to my now-empty glass. "I do have this coping mechanism."

Almost a decade of self-discovery and regular TIFF attendance later, there's a greater than zero percent chance that I'll wind up in the same situation, do the same thing and say the same thing this year.

If we are going to try to help autistic people with substance abuse issues, we can't stop at treating the addictions and compulsions themselves. It's great that professionals have now established that there is a problem, and that it affects us at a different rate than the non-autistic population. It's absolutely vital that anyone who wants to look into how to treat autistic people with addiction issues addresses the different ways that our brains and our social skills might respond to more traditional treatments—and what might need to be done differently to make sure that people aren't falling through the cracks as a result. But we also need to ask what is inspiring so many of us to experiment. And, frankly, *if* anyone has any better options. Because as long as being autistic in this world is so physically, emotionally and spiritually exhausting and confusing, we're going to need *something* to help us get through the day.[48]

---

48 The very act of trying to explain this kind of makes me want a drink.

STEP NINE

Fail

AUTISM DOESN'T JUST GIVE ME THE ABILITY TO OBSESSIVELY focus on narrow areas of interest for hours—or years—on end. Sometimes it also gives me narrow areas of sub-interest *within* those narrow areas of interest over which I can pore and perseverate!

I was fascinated by fitness in general when I started studying to become a personal trainer in my mid-twenties, but the more I learned, the more I began to zone in on very specific areas. The struggle between stability and mobility in the scapular[49] joint captivated me, and wanting to learn how to better address a healthy balance in this lone wolf of a joint was a major influence on my choice to become a Pilates instructor. I also had a phase where I spent a disproportionate amount of time wondering if the absence of a psoas minor—a small muscle that plays a role in pelvic movement performed from the quadruped position that is present in only 40 percent of humans—affects sexual performance at all. And I became extremely intrigued by chronic

....

49 Shoulder blade. Sure, I could have said "shoulder blade" to begin with, but I haven't put in thirty-eight years of autism and ten years of ongoing fitness education just to talk like a normal person.

overuse injuries, particularly those that seem to come as a complete surprise to the person suffering from it.

In general terms provided to you by a person who let their fitness studies lapse years ago, it goes like this: You can be doing something that's completely dysfunctional for years without noticing it. Something can be slightly off about the alignment of your knee, for example, in a way that causes no immediate or tangible pain. The movement just slightly tweaks something that's not exactly where it should be. On its own, this could be no big deal, but that same pattern, repeated over and over again for a long period of time, can take its toll. A tendon or ligament can become weakened and strained as it's brushed against the bone in a way it was never intended to, until one day, it can no longer withstand the wear and tear. That basic, simple movement you've done so many times before with no hint of a problem can suddenly shock you with a pop, a snap or a surge of pain. It will probably seem like a fluke injury. You just stepped off a curb and tore your MCL! But it took years of overcompensation and unwitting neglect to reach this surprise breaking point.

At the time that I was obsessed with this phenomenon, I was woefully unaware that the same thing was about to happen to my brain.

Becoming a personal trainer—and subsequently becoming a group fitness, spin and Pilates instructor—was my first big attempt to have a normal life. I was genuinely interested in working out and really enjoyed digging into the theory behind how our bodies work and how and why to make them move in certain ways for a desired result. I got a kick out of nerding out about stuff like the aforementioned "banging muscle," as I liked to call it, too. But going into it as a potential career was very much a compromise. The PFL had fizzled. My freelance writing career was stalled because I couldn't figure out the pitching process to save my life. Compared to pillow fighting and music journalism, fitness seemed like a stable and lucrative industry. I was trying to be a grown-up.

So I was already a little drained and dejected even before I started sucking at it. I was great at the theory, and good at applying it in a controlled environment. I did well in trial sessions where my fellow students or volunteer friends and family members served as my clients, and passed all of my practical exams. Something started to fall apart when I tried to translate everything I'd learned and practiced so hard into actual paying work, though.

My workout plans were sound. I know this, because I was still obsessively geeky about that part of the job. But I was only intermittently useful at one-on-one training. Group classes were even worse, as I struggled to find the right balance between personal attention and public speaking that they seemed to require.

I didn't really think of myself as a type A perfectionist at that point in my life—I figured anyone who bottoms out of academics and becomes a fake scholar in a pillow fighting league loses any right to that claim—but my complete inability to excel in my new venture still unmoored me. I hadn't managed to make much money or gain any attention in my previous gigs, but at least I'd been decent at the actual work I put in as a writer or performer. In fitness, I was just flat out unable to do something that everyone wanted from me. My bosses believed in my knowledge base and programs, but about 92 percent of the people taking my classes just couldn't connect with me. Most politely drifted to other options. Some complained about my lack of engagement with them, particularly when it came to eye contact.

Lacking any real context for why any of this might be happening, I chalked it all up to personal and moral failing. I was just too shy, and needed to come out of my shell more. I wasn't trying hard enough. I just needed to do more and work more, and Get Myself Out There, whatever that meant. I beat myself up harder in an effort to atone for what I'd done or failed to do so far. I pushed myself harder in an effort to stop being such a fuckup.

I dragged my frantic, demoralized ass all over Toronto, taking two buses and a subway to teach an indoor cycling class in a gym located at the back of a North York parking lot before sunrise, taking another bus and subway to oversee a boot camp in a hospital at lunch and a subway and a streetcar to a private session in the evening. (Like about 40 percent of autistic people, I don't drive. Like many un- or underemployed autistic people, I couldn't afford a car in Toronto even if I did.) I'd lug spare outfits and small equipment with me all day, changing and cleaning up where I could, going over and over my sessions and playlists in my head, choking down my rising panic and trying to calm a heart rate that climbed higher at the thought of teaching than it did when I was doing the exercises myself. Despite everything I'd heard about hard work paying off, though, neither my situation nor I improved much.

My life outside of work wasn't going that swimmingly, either. I got engaged, which was a truly joyous development (once I realized it wasn't a joke). I had friends I adored and who cared about me, too. My parents continued to be the very best. But I was also starting to have trouble keeping up with all of these people I loved so much and I lived in almost constant fear of losing them. I could never entirely shake the feeling that they would eventually figure out whatever it was about me that had turned everyone else against me in the past.

My one attempt at having a hobby that might improve my life and character was a mixed bag too. Signing up for Brazilian jiu-jitsu and Muay Thai lessons introduced me to even more amazing people to love and constantly worry about, but it also became another source of confused failure. I kept telling myself that working at something I wasn't naturally adept at was good for me, and that I'd eventually see improvements if I worked hard enough, but I think the best skill I learned during that period was how to stealth cry in a communal shower.

You might think, given this description of ongoing general mental malaise, that I did not, in fact, think that everything was going okay. But I did kind of think that was as good as it got, for all but the richest and most fortunate. Everyone from Viktor Frankl to Avril Lavigne was telling me that to live was to suffer and life was just like that, so I assumed what I was going through was what everyone went through. Besides, I'd grown up thinking that I might never find friends or love—or escape my hometown at all. I *was* living a life beyond my dreams.

I was about 99.2 percent sure that I was autistic by then, but I remained unsure there was anything I should—or could—do about it. I'd google testing and treatment options, but there was, as far as I could tell, nothing available for adults that was covered by Ontario's health care. If there was, it was definitely inaccessible enough that an extremely internet-savvy person like me couldn't figure out the appropriate steps to take toward it. There were clinics that offered private assessments and therapy, but I felt safe in assuming that they were out of my price range. Because almost everything was.

I was also, for some reason I still can't explain or defend, still under the bizarre impression that I was "cured." That I'd clearly checked off all of the boxes for "high-functioning" autism in childhood and adolescence, but that I'd grown out of most of those symptoms, and was fine now. As much as I wanted to get tested for the sake of better understanding where I'd come from—and maybe even for the sake of giving myself a break for how strange and unlikeable I'd been—I thought of it as more of a self-indulgence than a necessity. I figured I should save any resources that might have been available for the people with real problems.

And then I had a real problem.

It was a perfectly average day in the spring of 2009, arguably one of my lower stress ones. My future mother-in-law was coming into town to check out a museum exhibit and was going to meet my fiancé, Aaron, for lunch. He was going to call me when her plans were more solidified, and then I could figure out where and when to meet up with them.

I didn't have any classes or clients that day, but I was busy planning future sessions, piecing together appropriate playlists and toiling away at one of my occasional writing assignments. For reasons I no longer remember, my mom—essentially the only person I am happy to receive an impromptu phone call from—called on our landline. (Yes, we still had a landline and still do. We are old and set in our ways, please leave us be.) Mom and I got carried away and chatted because that's what we do and it was a welcome break from all of the overthinking and stressing I was doing as part of my natural working processes, and I forgot that I was waiting for another call.

Aaron repeatedly tried to call and text me, but we'd recently cancelled call waiting and I was such an innocent naïf in my pre-smartphone addiction days that I had, as per usual, forgotten to turn my cellphone on. By the time Aaron was able to get through to me, they were already at the restaurant. Thanks to the whims of the Toronto Transit Commission, I wasn't even able to make it in time for dessert or a post-meal greeting, either. To them, this was, at worst, a bummer. Aaron was fleetingly annoyed at the circumstances and my forgetfulness, but not angry. He acknowledged that the planning hadn't been ideal, anyway, and told me to forget about it.

I couldn't.

I'm miserable at forgiving myself for making mistakes and even worse at moving on from them. One of my first memories involves mistaking my uncle for my father when I was three. They both had the same red Chuck Taylors at the time, but I wasn't aware of that. I simply walked into a crowd of adults during a family event, saw the shoes and said, "Daddy, pick me up!" Everyone laughed, because good-natured laughter at kids' foibles is a thing that normal people do. But I was mortified, and I've never stopped regretting that mistake. Why didn't I look up? Why wouldn't I assess a situation before blurting something out? How could I have exposed myself to laughter like that? Even now, thirty-four years after the incident, and approximately thirty-three years, eleven months and thirty days after everyone else forgot about it (except my parents, who still have to listen to me dwell on this humiliating failure), the very act of recounting it is making my shoulders tense and my stomach churn.

My ability to deal with perfectly average human error in any way that is remotely appropriate or healthy had only deteriorated from there. So this wasn't just a mistake to me. It wasn't just an act of carelessness or distraction on my part that might require just a bit of reflection, and maybe a look into how I might be able to better remember and manage time and pending commitments in the future. It was bad. So I was bad.

The fallout from a Sarah Kurchak mistake can be roughly determined by the following equation:

Damage (Did I cause anyone actual harm? If so, how much, and is it at all forgivable?)

Times what my brain has decided the mistake *means*. (A reflection on my capability as a professional, or an adult in general? An example of how I never learn anything and always screw up in the end? A mark against my worth as a human being? A referendum on my right to exist at all?)

To the power of whatever else might be going on in my life. (Work stress? Career angst? Personal issues? The looming threat of complete failure across the board? Hormones? Everything just being too fucking loud all the time? A neurological condition that you're pretty sure you have but can't confirm and, therefore, you don't truly understand the full range of ways in which it might impact your life, let alone how you might begin to address those issues?)

And its progression generally follows the same pattern: I make a mistake. I react poorly to it. Before I can take the time to properly process what has happened, what it might mean and what I should do, my mind is already racing with worst-case scenarios. Then it gets stuck in a repetitive loop. Even if I do manage to recognize that my thought process is starting to spiral, there's nothing I can do to stop it at this point. It's like a broken record skipping over and over and over and over the same self-loathing sound bite. At some point, the tears, the choked breathing and the suicidal ideation kick in. If it's particularly bad, self-harm sneaks in, too.

The fallout from this particular fuckup was an omnishambles of all of the above and probably a bunch of other stuff that I have yet to work on or even identify, which eventually attached itself to one inescapable train of thought: My failure to remember the lunch date, my failure to properly prepare to receive further information about the lunch date and my failure to actually make the lunch date at all were a failure of organization, a failure of care and a failure of commitment on my part. I was failing to make a good impression on my soon-to-be family and would continue to fail in my future efforts to become a part of their world. I would fail at being a wife like I'd failed at everything else. Because I was a failure at keeping up my end of the bargain and contributing to society. I was a failure at being a proper part of a family. I was a failure at being here at all.

I tried to explain this to my mother in a series of increasingly inarticulate and self-loathing texts. Then I fired off one more: "I don't want to die. I just don't feel like I can earn the right to exist at all."

I threw the phone. I threw some other things. I hit the wall. I hit some other things. Mom called and I promised that I would hold on until she could get there. I did.

When the worst of it was over, she said that it was time to start the testing process. I objected, pointing out that none of us could afford it, but she waved it off. "We'll figure out something," she soothed. "Whether you are or you aren't, it will help us to know what we're working with here."

I broke down again after that. This time with relief and gratitude.

After a brief stint on a waiting list, I booked a series of appointments for an assessment at the Redpath Centre, a private mental health organization located in Toronto. As far as we could tell, it was well respected, and one of the few places of its kind in the country that seemed to offer comprehensive options for adults with neurodevelopmental issues. It was also located so close to my home that the act of going there didn't feel entirely insurmountable to me in my weakened state. Mom accompanied me to provide moral support and an outside perspective on any details of my early childhood I might need help with during the evaluation process.

I took a bunch of tests, filled out questionnaires, spent a lot of fun time digging through my past and picking apart my present concerns. As we were wrapping up, my assessor asked one final question: "What is your impression of me, Sarah?"

I went completely blank. Everything up until that point had made sense, and followed a pattern I could have predicted based on past therapy attempts and what I'd been able to google about the process to help prepare myself. Nowhere had I been given any hint that I'd have to deliver any sort of insight into a person I had only interacted with in such a structured, me-heavy format. So I said the first—okay, *only*— thing that came to mind.

"Well ... you've used my name a lot when we're speaking," I bumbled. "That shows me that you're really attentive."

At our next appointment, the assessor told me what I'd long suspected: I was autistic. Officially, at the time, I was told that I had Asperger's syndrome. He also believed I might have nonverbal learning disorder (a condition that's pretty much what it sounds like: a marked difference between verbal communication and visual-spatial abilities). There was another level of clinical testing we could have followed up with to confirm this diagnosis, but he didn't recommend it for my purposes. It was even more expensive and, given the dearth of services available for people with neurodevelopmental conditions over the age of eighteen in Ontario, unlikely to offer me any more than I already knew. After discussing it with my parents, we all felt that it was a better idea to put what little money we had left toward therapy instead.

If that sounds a bit anti-climactic, well ... I suppose it was. I'd spent years quietly desperate for answers. I'd spent most of that time thinking, or at least hoping, that those answers would be almost instantly transformative. Maybe concrete explanations for why I was the way I was would change the way that people approached me. Maybe some of them would appreciate what I was up against and how hard I'd been working to make myself acceptable and likeable to them, even if I hadn't actually accomplished it in the end, and at least factor my efforts into their assessments of my many failings. Maybe I could.

Spontaneous understanding and acceptance, I've since learned, are not hallmarks of the diagnostic process for adults. If we're lucky, we're mostly met with confusion. If we're not, it's suspicion or outright hostility. As one of the more fortunate members of my cohort, I was met with a lot of "You don't look autistic" and its twelve-inch remix, "You? Are you sure? Because I/my friend/my sister's boyfriend's sister's next-door neighbour know(s) this other autistic guy and he's, like, *really* autistic. He can't talk to girls." Some "I don't like labels." Usually with a side of "We label and diagnose everything these days." Occasionally with some concerns about "pharma" tossed in. There were a bunch of well-meaning puns about "Ass Burgers" and *Rain Man* jokes that I had to learn how to politely sidestep, because awkwardly responding to potentially sensitive issues and making them even more uncomfortable for everyone involved is not the sole domain of the autistic. And an assload of "I hope you don't use this as an excuse."

(Few, if any, of the omg No Excuses brigade can really articulate what they're truly concerned about. They never clarify what, specifically, they're afraid that I will use autism as an excuse *for*. Perhaps they mean my whole existence. Or that I'll use my diagnosis as a licence to be a free-ranging asshole. Or maybe rampant ableism has conditioned us all to believe that disabled people are just trying to get things handed to them, and anytime we find out that someone is disabled, we freak out and get ready to suspect them of scamming the precious system.)

Despite everyone's concerns that I might develop a case of sudden onset excuse-wielding, I remained unable to give myself any break whatsoever.

What my diagnosis lacked in epiphanies and eureka moments, it eventually made up for in slower-burning long-term assistance. I did acquire a more solid understanding of myself than what I'd managed to piece together before the testing. I also gained an excellent therapist who specialized in autistic adults and didn't believe in cures, or in treatments that encouraged the eradication of any outward signs of our condition. We worked on practical ways in which I could improve the quality of my life, and my ability to survive in this nonsense world. Whether I needed assistance in developing healthier day-to-day coping mechanisms, or a gentle nudge toward cultivating a modicum of self-acceptance, his knowledge base, ideology and patience were invaluable.

With this guidance, I was able to start working through my past and present. I eventually managed to forgive myself for a few things. I was also able to start sorting through what I actually wanted to work on and fix about myself versus what I simply wanted to learn how to accept. This is how I can now recognize the patterns and triggers that ganged up on me to lead to my meltdown that day, and why I can now describe them as well as I can. But that doesn't always mean that I can stop them when I see them coalescing again. At least not yet. I am still, ten years later, very much a work in progress. But at least I know what I'm working on now.

My diagnosis has absolutely become a net positive in my life. I have no idea where I would be now—or if I'd be here at all—if it hadn't happened. I'm truly grateful for the testing and subsequent treatment I've received, and incredibly lucky that it was only ("only") bank-breaking and not entirely out of reach financially. I'm so glad that, when one of the scariest and lowest moments of my life struck me out of nowhere, I had the emotional and monetary support that I needed to take this vital step toward some semblance of recovery.

But it never should have come to that.

Outcomes like mine appear to be the most common way that adults discover that they're autistic, next to spotting the signs in themselves after their child is diagnosed. I have no statistics to back this up,[50] but I've heard enough heartbreaking and harrowing stories from people who have reached out to me to believe that it's far from an isolated incident. Too many of us slip through the cracks. Too many of us push ourselves past our limits for years. Too many of us are unaware of what we're doing, what the cost might be or if there's any alternative. Too many of us break. Even if finally finding out or confirming that we are autistic helps, not enough of us will ever truly recover from what it took to make that discovery.

As long as the world we live in continues to prioritize how we appear over how we really are, and as long as seeming fine is confused with being fine, this will continue to happen. Autistic people who have any ability to conceal or hide— those of us who do not bother our normal counterparts too much—will be ignored. Those who can't will be trained to be more like those of us who can, and then they will be assumed to be fine and ignored as well. We'll be punished harshly for any slip in that appearance. It won't be until we crumble

....
50 This is another aspect of autistic life that has been left to anecdata.

completely under the pressure that anyone—maybe including ourselves—will realize how desperate our situation really is. And then we'll be faced with the challenge of living in a world that wasn't built for people like us *and* the challenge of trying to recover and rebuild.

(This is why I now support people who are self-diagnosed as autistic. Sure, that can and does lead to some bored average weirdos carelessly mimicking an identity and disability because they think it might make them look different or cool. Although not nearly at the rate that the anti-self-dx crowd would have you believe. But it also enables people from all walks of life who can't get diagnosed—or can't afford to—to better understand and take care of themselves. When I think of how different my own life might have been if I'd allowed myself to actually think of myself as autistic when I first suspected, without expensive external permission to do so, I think risking some potential annoying posturing from the former population is worth it to save the lives of the latter.)

When so-called "high-functioning" autistic people who might appear to be fine to the untrained eye speak out about the importance of acceptance for autistic people, we're not trying to argue that autism is just cute or quirky, or no big deal. Some of the struggles I've described so far might not be as severe as what many autistic people face, but that doesn't mean they were mild. They still led to my crisis. They're still contributing to the confusion and misery I'm muddling through after it. When we bring up the need for treatments and support that are more about helping us thrive as we are as opposed to just making it look like we are, we're not doing so because we think these things are easy. It's because we know they're not. It's because we have been through things that we wouldn't wish on any other human being. And because we believe that all autistic people are human beings, that means that we want better for all of us.

No one should be punished for looking too okay, or for suffering too much in silence. The cost of actual help shouldn't be so high—and I mean that financially, physically and emotionally. No one should have to feel their entire life spiral out of control in a single moment just because they haven't paid that price yet. No one should be left so entirely in the dark as to what is happening to them or how they can stop it. No one should feel like they have no right to stop it— or that everyone would be better off if they didn't. No one who survives that should be forced to pick up the pieces and rebuild when the same fault lines that brought about the last scare are still there, still not entirely charted.

Now, in my experience as an autistic person and as a writer who has tried to bring more attention to certain aspects of the autistic experience, I have noticed that there can be a gap in the ways that autistic readers and non-autistic readers receive ideas like the one above. For all of your vaunted empathy, my dear non-auts, some of you aren't great at putting yourselves in our shoes. Many of you can imagine caring for someone like us—or at least being near one of us—but imagining yourself *as* us can be a step too far.

So I'm going to restate this from a different perspective, just to make sure my point is as clear as possible to as many people as possible.

No parents, who have done everything within and beyond their resources to protect and care for their child, should ever be confronted with the harsh reality of how little those efforts can help when they're thrown up against everything else their child will face in life. No parents should feel their hearts and stomachs drop when they get those phone calls or texts that let them know just how dangerous things are getting for their loved one again. No parents should have to rush to their adult child's side, unsure of what they can do when they get there, but just hoping they can make it in time. No parents should have to live in anticipation of the next call.

STEP TEN

Discover that GI Joe lied and knowing is not always half the battle

I AM NOT A BIG FAN OF SIMPLE, STRAIGHTFORWARD MENTAL health narratives. I'm thrilled for anyone whose recovery has been relatively linear and I get why they want to share their stories. It's admirable that people who have made it through some shit want to decrease stigma and give hope to anyone still in it. But any time I see a public figure or personal acquaintance contribute to an awareness campaign with some variation of "I had anxiety/depression, but I reached out to friends/called a helpline/saw a medical professional. I went on medication/got therapy/talked it through with supportive loved ones, and I'm okay now," I feel equally envious and mystified.

You mean to tell me that you had a problem, identified the problem, asked for help, got it, treated your problem ... and got better? What is this witchcraft?

When my assessor confirmed that I was autistic, my immediate thought was, *Now that we know, we can fix it.* When my therapist explained that he didn't believe in fixing autism, and starting laying out what we could focus on in our sessions instead, I thought, *Even better. I'll therapy and healthy coping mechanism my heart out (and medicate if necessary) and still be me but without all of the depression and anxiety!*

It turns out there is no such clear path between A and B when A equals "twenty-seven years of confusion, overloaded senses, trauma and maladjustments recently uncovered as the result of a crisis."

I had an aptitude for the introspection and self-awareness part of my therapy, but my ability to apply any of what I was discovering or better understanding to my life was suboptimal. My therapist started to hear a lot of variations of "logically I know that ___, *but* ..." Like "logically I know that anyone who would reject me for being myself isn't worth my time or effort, but I can't stop desperately trying to court their approval because I am so afraid of being attacked and/or alone again." And "logically I know that I will not find any valuable information about self-improvement from gossip boards and that the act of lurking on them is increasing my anxiety and decimating what's left of my fragile self-esteem, but every time I try to stop, I get anxious that I'm missing valuable information about self-improvement and I'll become an even more loathsome piece of garbage."[51]

In the weeks and months that followed my diagnosis, I was able to start identifying the many, many things that I had been doing to obscure my autistic nature. I was surprised to discover just how many hacks I'd developed. And a little shocked when my therapist informed me that they weren't perfectly common behaviours that everyone does all the time. I *logically, but*-ed my way through any substantial efforts to alter these habits, too, but I figured talking about them was almost as good. If I couldn't improve the quality of my life, I could at least improve the quality of all of those

....

51 I really can't exaggerate how often those bloody message boards have come up.

dreadful "but you don't look autistic" conversations I was getting stuck in.

My ideal script for these engagements looked something this:[52]

Person and Me: (*Engaging in pleasant conversation that leads to a place where I feel it would be appropriate and comfortable to say that I'm autistic.*)

Me: I'm autistic.

Person: Really? You don't look autistic.

Me: I've been looking at your eyebrows to make it look like I'm actually looking into your eyes this whole time. [Leaving out the part where there's a good chance that my gaze probably drifted to their teeth at some point, probably got stuck there, and then I had to worry about how I had become fixated on yet another person's mouth when I try so hard to avoid this particular habit of mine. And worry about whether they've noticed that I am staring at their mouth, all while trying to keep up with the conversation and all of my other tricks.] I've been tapping my right foot against the floor, because I've managed to turn most of my repetitive movement patterns into things that non-autistic people also do and are therefore seen as normal expressions of energy/excitement/boredom/nerves. I've probably been playing with my hair for the same reason.

The tone of my voice is modelled after my mom's, although I've probably picked up some other

....
52   "Meticulously drafting and rehearsing potential things to say in conversations" was one of those behaviours that I was shocked to find out wasn't as common as, say, blinking.

subconscious influences from all of the TV shows and movies I watched to try to augment my middlingly developed social skills. The way I talk with my hands is 100 percent my mom. I have no idea if they're helpful. I don't think my gestures are in any way connected to what I'm actually saying. But she talks with her hands and people love her, so I started doing it and now it just kind of happens. The structure and content of this conversation were probably culled from similar sources.

I have at least four different tracks running through my brain while we're talking. One is trying to make sure my fake eye contact makes me look attentive but not creepy. [Omitting the track dedicated to the teeth thing.] One is following our conversation, and trying to process what you're saying and come up with thematically relevant responses in return. One is making sure that I'm not monopolizing the conversation and that I'm asking you an appropriate number of appropriate questions in return. One is trying to keep me from saying something weird. It's probably failing. On top of all that, I'm trying to tune out all of the background noise—including, but not limited to: cars, other conversations, breathing, chewing, possible music being pumped out of a speaker somewhere and buzzing lights—in order to hear what you're saying.

There's a lot I'm probably leaving out. I'll probably realize this at around four a.m. when I'm not sleeping and kick myself, and then not sleep some more because I'm worried that I have failed to successfully illustrate how autistic I am and how hard I have worked to now get to the point where I have to prove that I am all of the things I am trying to spare you from.

Person: That sounds hard.

Me: It can be challenging! [Exits to nearest public washroom that doesn't smell too much of industrial cleaner or lack thereof and isn't overrun by constantly howling high-tech hand driers to hang out in a stall and breathe and/or cry into my hands for a while. Or go home to half-consciously stare at a screen, fail to nap and have a good fetal position moment. Or some other amenable time out to allow for recovery from the interaction.][53]

When I could manage to get it out of my brain and mouth, this rambling awareness campaign had a decent success rate. Covering most of my script over a coffee with one friend led to a relationship heart-to-heart.

"Sometimes when we're talking, you start looking elsewhere. I thought maybe you were getting bored," she said.

"I do that because I'm comfortable with you!" I replied. "And because I get really into what we're talking about and I can follow it better if I'm not worried about eye contact." We've been great ever since.

Other times doing the work described in the script left me too sapped to say it. I had a rough go reviewing films at TIFF 2016[54] for one of the websites I write for. One of my best friends called me with a medium-level problem on opening night. I was only a third of my way into my first assignment and rapidly approaching my deadline, but I didn't know how to tell her that. So I let her talk it out, did the best I could to provide that valuable advice I used to give, cried out of deadline panic and an inability to compartmentalize my friend's emotions, under-slept,

. . . .

53 These steps can also be employed in the event of a dismissal or accusation of faking.
54 If you're wondering why all of my recent awkward anecdotes have happened during the Toronto International Film Festival, it's because these days that's the only time I consistently leave home to do things alone.

filed my imperfect review at the last minute and never recovered from that deficit for the rest of the festival. From then on, everything was too loud. The emotions I was watching onscreen were overwhelming me. I couldn't navigate crowds or articulate my thoughts. While taking a break at a nearby pub between screenings, I found out that my aunt's dog had died and openly wept into my salad because I felt so terrible for her.

At the closing brunch, I got chatting with an acquaintance of an acquaintance—and fellow long-term TIFF-goer—about how we both felt more drained this year than usual. I mentioned that I was struggling with some my autism-related issues more than I had in festivals past.

"You're autistic?" she said, not unkindly. "I never would have known!"

I had the script. I also had a collection of mental and written notes I'd been keeping throughout the festival with the idea of eventually turning the experience into an essay on the amount of work that goes into not looking autistic.[55] But all that came out in the moment was "Oh. Okay."

In the years of therapy, self-reflection and trading stories with my fellow autistic people that followed, I gained a deeper understanding of these things I was doing and explaining with varying degrees of success—and I learned that I was not alone. Some of the particulars and how I came to develop them might be unique to me, but the behaviour itself is a common one for a sizeable percentage of autistic

....

55 I never did write the essay. Thanks, executive dysfunction! But here are some highlights from the notes: "Bad writing night." "Meltdown at Convention Centre??" "Convinced I'm the worst." "Dead dog bar sadness." "Panic." "Paranoia." "Italian critic only talked about self."

people. Such efforts to camouflage any obvious signs of our autism is called masking.

Masking is yet another under-examined aspect of autistic existence. Studies on the topic are in their infancy, and the scope of the research is far from optimal. Which means the findings are, too. And they have yet to meaningfully address important factors like race, class and gender. (Work in this field has started to look into the differences between autistic men and women when it comes to camouflaging, for example, but how useful are observations rooted in the gender binary when we already know that autistic people are more likely to be gender non-conforming than our peers?[56]) Their working definitions of masking are vague at best. One 2017 study, "Quantifying and Exploring Camouflaging in Men and Women with Autism,"[57] loosely explains masking as a difference between how someone appears in social contexts and what's happening on the inside.

From this wading pool of knowledge that does not adequately address the diversity of experiences, identities and needs in the autistic population, the best I can do is piece together this general overview:

There does seem to be some gender disparity when it comes to masking.[58] This isn't to say that no boys or men engage in the behaviour, but researchers have noted that their autistic female subjects tend to participate in more and deeper versions of it. I suspect that similar differences can probably be found in any autistic population that isn't perfectly in line with what is still treated as the norm by too

....

56   Bryony White, "The Link Between Autism and Trans Identity," *The Atlantic* (November 15, 2016). See https://www.theatlantic.com/health/archive/2016/11/the-link-between-autism-and-trans-identity/507509/.

57   M.C. Lai et al., "Quantifying and Exploring Camouflaging in Men and Women with Autism," *Autism* (2017) 21(6): 690–702. See https://www.ncbi.nlm.nih.gov/pubmed/27899710.

58   Ibid.

many professionals. The less that society tolerates characteristics like rugged individuality, oddness, bluntness and behaviour that could be interpreted as aggression from someone of your race, gender, sexuality, abilities or economic situation, the more you'll need to hide any sign of them just to stay alive.

However, while masking can help autistic people survive in daily life, it can also prevent us from receiving the supports we need when we need them. Not only have we gone (relatively) unnoticed by our peers, we've managed to slip past the very people who are qualified to recognize and diagnose autism. Although there's no empirical proof yet, I believe it's possible that part of the reason the rate of diagnosed autism is so much higher in boys than in girls is at least partially related to autism experts failing to recognize the semi-successful camouflaging of diagnostic criteria. In some cases, we even manage to hide from ourselves. Many autistic people don't realize the extent of their own masking until they receive a diagnosis well into their adulthood and start looking back through their lives with this newfound perspective.

If we don't always notice its prevalence, though, we certainly notice its toll. "All of these strategies call for considerable effort," *Spectrum*'s Francine Russo wrote in the February 2018 article "The Costs of Camouflaging Autism."[59] "Exhaustion was a near-universal response in [quantifying and exploring camouflaging in men and women with autism]. The adults interviewed described feeling utterly drained—mentally, physically and emotionally. One woman ... explained that after camouflaging for any length of time, she needs to curl up in the fetal position to recover. Others said they feel their friendships are not real because they

....

59   Francine Russo, "The Costs of Camouflaging Autism," *Spectrum* (February 21, 2018). See https://www.spectrumnews.org/features/deep-dive/costs-camouflaging-autism/.

are based on a lie, increasing their sense of loneliness. And many said they have played so many roles to disguise themselves through the years that they have lost sight of their true identity."

Women in the study reported that controlling their repetitive behaviours (what we call "stimming") left them less able to handle their sensory issues and emotions. Masking can leave a person with less energy to handle other aspects of their day, from performing basic housework to processing thoughts and feelings. This, in turn, can lead to meltdowns and burnout. Something as simple as trying not to play with my hair or keeping my legs still while sitting in public can leave me depleted after a few hours.

There's little to no solid information on the effects of masking over the long term, but I suspect that this continued drain on our resources is at least partially responsible for the high rates of anxiety and depression among autistic people. It's possible that it could be connected to physical health problems, as well. And it wouldn't shock me to find out that it plays a role in the fact that autistic adults are nine times more likely to die by suicide than the general population.[60]

As much as I suffer from masking, and as much as I hate what it has done and is continuing to do to me, it would be careless of me to discuss this facet of some autistic lives entirely in terms of the negative impact of engaging in it and the benefits of stopping. There are as many issues with masking—and not masking—as there are autistic individuals.

Not everyone can mask. Nonverbal or preverbal autistic people cannot easily blend into a society that prioritizes talking above all other forms of communication. The ability to

---

60 Autistica, *Personal Tragedies, Public Crisis: The Urgent Need for a National Response to Early Death in Autism*. See http://www.sciencemag.org/sites/default/files/documents/AUTISTICA%20REPORT%20-%20Personal%20Tragedies%2C%20Public%20Crisis.pdf.

physically control our bodies enough to redirect or hide our atypical movements is far from universal. So is the cognitive function required to execute camouflaging. Masking might be destroying us, but it's also gained us access to a world that is denied to many of our fellow autistic human beings.

Not everyone can quit masking, either. In our racist society, for one particularly pressing example, a behaviour that might be tolerated when it's witnessed in a white autistic person could be interpreted as threatening when an autistic person of colour does the same thing. A white person who experiments with being more visibly autistic in public is taking a chance that they might be rejected and hurt by people who don't accept them as is, and the ramifications of this isolation can be severe. But we are not at the same risk of police brutality, abuse and death.

I'm privileged to be able to mask, and privileged to be in a place where I can even begin to consider stopping. Whatever I say or do about my own relationship to this behaviour, I think it's extremely important that I remain aware and considerate of this fact.

It's also not easy to separate what masking has cost me from what it's given me. It's unfortunate that I was bullied so badly that I felt the need to drastically alter so much of myself. When I was faced with that situation, though, at least I had the ability to try to change things. It wasn't a permanent solution, but it gave me a breathing period in which I was able to make a few friends and live in a little peace. It sucks that I wound up bullied and scared again when I started high school, but at least I could regroup and redouble my efforts at that point. It's sad that I spent the ass end of my adolescence home alone, watching movies and lurking on the internet, but at least it gave me the sheen of normality that allowed me to get back into the world, and have a shot at finally finding a weird little place for myself out there.

If it hadn't been for those periods of messy grace, I never could have made it to a point in my life where I could start to worry about the toll my efforts have taken on me. You can't address your raging identity crisis until your basic survival needs are taken care of. Masking might be one of the greatest threats to my existence now, but it's why I'm still here at all.

There's also the pesky little fact that I don't know *how* to stop.

Logically, I know that I probably can afford to strip away most of the masking behaviours I've detailed in this book so far. I have loved ones who, after hearing some version of my script, have told me that I don't need to do any of those things around them, and I believe them. I have jobs I can do from home, where I don't have to worry about fitting into workplace culture. I don't have to go out in public regularly, so I don't have to worry much about how I'll be perceived there. And everything from the meltdowns I'm having over minor faux pas to my alarmingly high resting heart rate is telling me that I should cut back for my mental and physical well-being.

But I'm still trying to figure out how and where I'd start.

I don't know how to temper a lifetime of high-alert survival instincts, no matter how poorly formed and detrimental they might be. I don't know how to unlearn all of these tricks that I bludgeoned into myself until they became ingrained, no matter how much they take out of me every time I reflexively try them. Making or mimicking eye contact can suck the life out of me, but sometimes I don't realize I'm attempting it until I start to feel the strange full-body discomfort the action gives me. I'm not entirely sure I've even figured how deep these camouflaging behaviours run yet.

I used to think that writing was one place where I could be truly sure I was myself, for example. But in the process of writing this book, I've begun to wonder if I'm doing a variation of all of my old tricks here, too. I feel almost as confused and isolated in a field dominated by non-autistic writers and editors as I did on the playground. In addition to the normal professional development—and the occasional indulgence in petty jealousy—that any good writer should pursue, I obsessively monitor what kind of stories from what kind of writers seem to appeal to readers. I try to figure out *why* those things appeal to others and then pick at my psyche until it bleeds something closer to that ideal. I do my best to contort my work into a voice that will have some kind of purchase in the non-autistic discourse, substituting replacing eye contact with word choices and body language and tone for, well, tone. I've slipped back into the habit of trying to anticipate every possible negative outcome in the hopes of offsetting them.

Maybe what I'm doing is normal and making me a better writer. Maybe it's unhealthy and breaking me. Or maybe it's both. It'll probably be years before I start to untangle how it could be benefiting me, how it could be ruining my life further, and what, if anything, I can do to change. I'm guessing it will take longer still before I can manage to implement any of those potential course corrections.

It's not like, as the term "masking" seems to evoke, there's a superficial layer of actions and appearances that I can remove and instantly improve my life. I don't have a mask I can remove; I have a multiheaded, deeply embedded parasite. It's probably killing me, but it's also kept me alive, and I don't know how much of it I can remove and still survive. I'm not completely sure where it ends and I begin at this point.

And again, I have it pretty easy compared to so many of my fellow autistic people.

There's nothing straightforward or simple about any of this.

STEP ELEVEN

Write a story about vaccines.
Never hear the end of it

NO ONE SHOULD HAVE TO SEE THEMSELVES USED AS A BOOGEY-man in an evidence-free conspiracy theory that leads to increasingly frequent public health scares. But I'm hard-pressed to think of a population less equipped to handle being dragged into such an absurd and dangerous mess than autistic people. And yet here we are.

Once upon a time in 1998 the con artist formerly known as *Dr.* Andrew Wakefield published a study in a medical jour-nal called *The Lancet* that single-handedly convinced the world that vaccines cause autism. The only problem with this game-changing revelation was that it wasn't true.[61] No one else has been able to reproduce the results of this study or to prove any connection between vaccines and autism. Wakefield's paper was questioned in 2004 and fully refuted in 2010. (Among other concerns, Wakefield was revealed to have deep financial ties to lawyers and families who were suing vaccine manufacturers. Some of their kids were, in

....
61   A.J. Wakefield et al., "RETRACTED: Ileal-Lymphoid-Nodular Hyperplasia, Non-Specific Colitis, and Pervasive Developmental Disorder in Children," *The Lancet* (February 28, 1998). See https://www.thelancet.com/journals/lancet/article/PIIS0140-6736(97)11096-0/fulltext.

fact, subjects of his study. There is also a possibility that he paid for blood samples at his son's birthday party, although he now claims he was only joking when he described these ace research techniques at a 1999 talk at the MIND Institute of the University of California.[62])

These pesky facts have not stopped a certain segment of the population—mostly rich, privileged white people whose lives are almost entirely immunized from the consequences of their actions in general—from running with the idea that vaccines cause autism. Or that they might cause autism. In either case, they figure that getting your child vaccinated isn't worth the risk. Now all sorts of fun things like measles and whooping cough are making comebacks. Despite anti-vaxxers' insistence that these are minor illnesses and no big deal, people have died as a result of these outbreaks. And people will continue to suffer and die from completely preventable illnesses. All because an abstract, imaginary threat of autism scares a chunk of the population more than the real-life threat of death and disease.

Imagine that you have a neurodevelopmental disability that gives you some challenges with social skills and possibly the occasional rigid adherence to things like truth and fairness. Chances are good that you've been explicitly and implicitly told that you are pedantic, rude, blunt and not considerate enough of others' points of views for your whole life.

Now picture this: You are told that people are dying because spoiled rich assholes are afraid to vaccinate their kids because a discredited former doctor—who either buys children's blood at birthday parties or at least thinks it's appropriate to joke about buying kids' blood for research purposes—told them that the autism fairy will visit their kids

....
62   Owen Dyer, "Wakefield Admits Fabricating Events When He Took Children's Blood Samples," *British Medical Journal* (April 19, 2008) 336 (7649): 850. See https://www.ncbi.nlm.nih.gov/pmc/articles/PMC2323045/.

if they get them vaccinated. Because, well, when it comes down to it, they'd much rather risk having a dead child than offspring who are anything like you.

Now imagine trying to employ all of those social skills that might not come naturally to you in order to fake some semblance of politeness and tolerance in the face of that incredibly wrong and hurtful fuckery.

Well, I wrote a slightly more polite and rigorously cited version of the above paragraphs for an online publication called *Archipelago* in February 2015 and I'm still dealing with the fallout of that on a regular basis.

"I'm Autistic, And Believe Me, It's A Lot Better Than Measles"[63] was only the second professional piece that I wrote about autism after my diagnosis (and the first of many that wound up with some variation of "I'm Autistic And ..." or "I Have Autism And ..." in the headline). I'd put together a listicle of autistic and autistic-coded TV characters for a pop culture outlet and dabbled with a blog I dubbed "Awesometism," but this was my first serious effort at tackling my brain and body and our place in the world. I was frustrated by the way autistic people were being harmed by a situation that should never have involved us to begin with, and angry that almost no one seemed keen to seek out our perspective at all. I wanted to contribute my only skill to the cause in the only way I knew how. When an editor and writer I admired said that she was looking for an autistic writer to tackle the topic, I leapt at the chance.

Almost immediately upon publication, it became the biggest story I'd ever written.

I was not naive to the ways of the internet by any means. I'd been online since I was a teenager and I'd been writing

....

63 Sarah Kurchak, "I'm Autistic, And Believe Me, It's A Lot Better Than Measles," *Archipelago* (February 6, 2015). See https://medium.com/the-archipelago/ im-autistic-and-believe-me-its-a-lot-better-than-measles-78cb039f4bea.

about all-important polarizing topics like music, movies and mixed martial arts for almost a decade and a half at that point. And I'd been doing all of the above *as a woman*. While I considered myself lucky compared to many of my colleagues—particularly women of colour, who face exponentially more abuse online—I'd still received my fair share of abusive messages and threats. I knew how mean and vile people could be. I just wasn't prepared for how mean and vile they would be in this specific way on this specific issue.

The nice anti-vaxxers called me a shill for Big Pharma. The less charitable among them concluded that I was a poor, vaccine-damaged pawn who had been manipulated by Big Pharma to spew their lies. These responses weren't entirely unexpected, but they annoyed me all the same. They weren't just calling into question my integrity when they called me a sellout, I joked to friends, they were severely underestimating my price!

Laughing off the rest got harder, especially when it started to feel like I was letting people from what was supposed to be my own community down.

"Congratulations on your superlative writing skills," an early comment by the parent of an autistic child seethed. "My son has never written anything quite so eloquent as your propaganda piece."

"If you're able to make your own informed decisions about your own health and welfare, then yes, you're in pretty good shape," another commenter quickly added. "However a great many individuals with autism have communication and cognitive deficits that will reduce their quality of life. They can't communicate their needs, they can't advocate for their own care and they'll be condemned to a life of physical pain and discomfort unless we find some way to reverse this disease. I understand that medicine places both slightly disabled and extremely disabled people on the same causal spectrum, but that doesn't mean that what is right for you is right for all who have the diagnosis."

"PFFT," another concurred. "If somebody is self aware enough to say they have Autism. THEY DO NOT HAVE AUTISM."

These three comments, received in the early hours of my thirty-third birthday, were my introduction to Autism Warrior Parents. AWP is a term coined by Shannon Des Roches Rosa—a writer and autistic ally who is the parent of a son with high support needs but is not, herself, an Autism Warrior Parent—to describe a subset of the autism community who tend to believe that voices like mine are inherently detrimental to their cause.

"Autism Warrior Parents aren't limited to the typical post-Jenny McCarthy-era diehards who—despite the unequivocal debunking of any link between autism and vaccines—still consider their autistic kids vaccine-damaged rather than, in the words of writer and autistic parent Carol Greenburg, 'neurologically outnumbered,'" Des Roches Rosa wrote for *The Establishment* on the subject in 2016.[64] "They also include those who fund or promote questionable autism science, and parents who consider their children so impaired that the opinions and personal experiences of autistic activists are irrelevant to them—that, in other words, any autistic adult who can put words on a screen or speak must have fewer support needs than their own autistic children and should therefore be ignored. At the root, Autism Warrior Parents are those who, for whatever reason, refuse to accept their autistic child's actual reality and needs, and instead put their energies into absolute change or control of that child."

....

64 Shannon Des Roches Rosa, "How 'Autism Warrior Parents' Harm Autistic Kids," *The Establishment* (September 22, 2016). See https://medium.com/the-establishment/how-autism-warrior-parents-harm-autistic-kids-6700b8bf6677.

Unaware that there were people out there who would never be convinced that I had anything valuable to say about autism, no matter how hard I tried, I blamed myself for these responses. If they were upset, then I obviously hadn't explained myself clearly enough. Maybe I hadn't properly articulated that I don't consider myself better than other autistic people. Or that I don't believe that an autistic person's value comes from their ostensible level of function, but from the fact that they are a human being. Maybe I hadn't been clear enough that, even though I might have certain privileges or advantages that not all autistic people have, I don't have it easy, either.

I didn't *think* I'd done that. There's a passage in the measles op-ed that says, "I have good days where my strange and intense interests give me a unique perspective in my writing and my focus helps me get it down on paper. I have bad days where I can't ride public transit without having a panic attack and I have to leave the room when my husband chews food because I find the sound of it unbearable and overwhelming. I have stimmed to my heart's content and I have hit myself. Throughout all but the worst of it—depression is a common comorbidity of autism, likely because living in the neurotypical world is often trying—I've been pretty sure that I am 'living,' and better for it. Throughout all of it, my loved ones have preferred my autism to my possible illness or death, or the deaths of others. I'd say I was grateful, but really, this should be a given." I thought that was I being pretty damned open and honest when I wrote it.

But now I worried that I hadn't gone far enough. So when more parents started emailing me and messaging me, criticizing my representation of autism and demanding to know more details about my own life, I thought that I owed them answers—and details. I wrote back to them guilelessly and earnestly—ironically, the very autism they accused me of not really having prevented me from even considering that they might have ulterior motives, or that I had a right to question them—and divulged parts of my life that I thought would help them realize that I might not know exactly what it's like to be their child, but I understand more than they might assume. I believed that this would make them appreciate that I was autistic enough to deserve a say, and that I was doing my best to fight for all of us.

No one changed their minds. The ones who did respond either rejected my secrets as still not enough, or they demanded even more of them. There are complete strangers in this world somewhere who now know things about me that even my closest friends don't know. And, even after reading my replies, they were still able to turn around and argue that I was either lying or misrepresenting myself. I received my first round of many accusations that I was "glamorizing autism" and was told that my words and my work were drawing attention away from their real tragedy and their real needs.

The praise I received for the story far outweighed the criticisms, but the positive responses began to drain me in their own way, too. The retweets, shares and likes were a welcome novelty to a writer who was still hungry for her first hints of external validation almost fifteen years into her career. It was an ego stroke to see that some people thought what I'd done was brilliant. After a while, though, it became clear to me that at least a percentage of the people who claimed to appreciate my story weren't any more invested in the well-being of autistics than my detractors were. My work had simply provided a convenient prop for their own campaigns against anti-science types.

The response from some of my fellow autistics made me worry that I'd missed the mark almost as much as the irate parents had. Every time someone felt the need to pepper a thank you with a description of how high their function was, how mild their autism was, and how great they were and how much they contributed to society, I wanted to scream that that wasn't the fucking point. It sickened me to think that I'd given any autistic person any fuel to help them think they were better than any other one of us, or that only some of our lives meant something.

It was the messages from people who got it, and who did make me feel like I'd accomplished something of value, that really broke me, though. The relief I felt when another autistic person recognized what I was actually trying to say quickly faded in the face of how desperately they were thanking me for making headway with the outside world at all. I was incredibly grateful for the support I started to receive from non-autistic moms—and it was almost always moms— as the article continued to gain traction, but their stories left me so completely heartbroken that I couldn't do more.

The moms I started to hear from during that period are the kind of people you hear about even less often than you hear from autistic people. They don't publish books about what a burden their children are, or run charities like Autism Speaks. These parents were so much like my own. They loved their children so much and all they wanted was the ability to minimize their struggles and help them survive in a world that wasn't built for them. They wrote to say that they found hope in me not because they perceived me as successful by normal people merits, but because I was an autistic person who tried to stand up for herself and tried to help her fellow people. Others shared loving testaments to their children. (One comment in particular is now permanently wedged in my heart: "As the mother of a son with autism, who died of complications after digestive tract surgery when he was twenty, I can say that living with his autism was much easier than living without him.") Some wanted to know if I had any suggestions, tips or words of encouragement for them.

I wrote back to the first few, but I was rapidly overwhelmed by the volume and passion of their missives. I didn't know how to say that I wished they had more support for their kids and for themselves. That I wished every autistic person had the opportunity to be seen through eyes like theirs. Or that, more than anything, I wished we weren't all just collateral damage in this vaccine war. Every time I tried, I just broke down in another round of exhausted tears.

Empathy is an even trickier subject in the autistic community than most. It's far too complicated a topic to satisfactorily tackle in the course of a single context-providing aside in an essay that's only slightly related, but I'll do my best: Autistic people are dismissed as lacking empathy or having none at all. Some autistic people have overcorrected this stereotype by arguing that we're all actually hyper-empathetic, and it only appears that we don't empathize because feeling others' emotions too strongly makes us shut down, or we don't express it the way non-autistic people do or can recognize. In reality, our ability to experience and process empathy is, like pretty much everything about us, as individual as we are. And empathy really isn't as important to being a good person as many non-autistic people seem to think it is. You don't have to empathize with someone to give a shit about them, or to help others. Sometimes too much empathy can make you kind of useless to others. At least mine does.

You know in *Star Trek Generations* when Data, the beloved logical android, is given an emotion chip and he initially falls apart and is unable to act in a moment of crisis because he doesn't know how to handle his emotions? That's basically my entire life. I quickly get overwhelmed by other people's feelings, and even if I want to help or reach out to them in some other way—which I often do—I'm too busy shutting down or curling up in the fetal position again to be of much use. Calls get dropped. Emails go unanswered. Things get left unsaid. Nothing is ever forgotten, though. The moments that inspired me to break down and my inability to do anything meaningful about them will both continue to keep me up at night for the rest of my life. But nothing is really ever helped, repaired or grown, either.

This makes dealing with strangers' emotions about my work, a challenge for any writer, exceptionally hard for me. With time, I have made some headway when it comes to topics other than autism. It might not be pleasant to deal with bitter anger directed at me for something I've written on pop culture or sports, but at least it's relatively straightforward to recognize, process and compartmentalize: People (mostly men) get mad that I have the temerity to have opinions on stuff they think is supposed to belong to them—and that I have a forum in which to express them—and they direct their generalized anxieties about what they feel is their diminishing place in the world onto me specifically. I react poorly at first, because being greeted with free-flowing bile for doing your job is always going to be bullshit. And then I move on because fuck them. Or I alert my editors to the situation if an actual threat is made, then try to move on.

The fallout from my autism work, however, comes from all directions and covers almost the entire spectrum (sorry) of human emotion. Logically, I can tell myself that not all of the emotional blowback I receive is really about me. Sometimes I'm just an accessible target for people, mostly Autism Warrior Parents, who have nowhere else to channel their fears, pains and exhaustions. They can't yell at abstract concepts like a lack of understanding, or a dearth of services and support, so they shoot off a nasty letter to someone they assume isn't struggling—and has never struggled—like they do. (A truly startling number of people assume that I am perfectly functional and doing well in life because I can write. As if this is a skill that requires or even encourages any level of normal humanity. As if the entire profession isn't overrun by dysfunctional messes of all neurologies.) Awareness of and sympathy for their motives can't do much to dampen the onslaught of barely filtered human experience that I've absorbed, though. Whether someone is trying to yell at me, hurt me as much as they hurt, undermine me, thank me, make a connection or spill their entire life story because, for the first time in their lives, they think there might be someone who understands, it all knocks me on my ass.

The details of topics, publications and exact characteristics of empathy-related issues might be unique to me, but I think what I've gone through in general is common for autistic writers who have chosen to reflect on any aspect of autism in their work. We put a piece of ourselves into the world knowing full well that part of our audience will find it wanting. Any boundaries that we try to establish for the sake of our privacy, or the privacy of subjects who have trusted us with a piece of their own story, will be treated as evasion or fabrication. People will try to make us pay for the sins of a system that also hurts us, no matter how much they'll try to claim otherwise. We'll be loved and hated, patronized and respected, and thanked and scolded. The vitriol of our detractors and the gratitude of our admirers will remind us of how heartbreakingly under-served and misunderstood autistic people are. And then we have to figure out how to even begin to process all of that. Usually on top of still dealing with whatever issue it was that we wrote about to begin with.

This has been my life since February 6, 2015. I don't want to complain too much, though. Part of the reason that I face this unfortunate series of circumstances on an almost daily basis is because I've had the privilege and the luck to be able to write about autism—and some other very serious things, like the relationship between my virginity and *Texas Chainsaw Massacre 2*—on a fairly regular basis since then. That story and its success helped me to make connections, successfully pitch more publications and start to assemble a bit of a portfolio. Essentially, it helped me get to a place where all of the parts of the job that I sucked at—the networking, the building of friendly professional relationships, the working up the guts to cold call people *and* follow-up—started to matter just a little less than the writing I was doing. I started to build the foundations of an actual writing career—only about fifteen years behind the schedule of many of my non-autistic colleagues.

The other reason that I've been stuck in this feedback loop, though, is because that original story just never seems to become any less relevant. Every time there's a new measles outbreak, the story's reach once again spreads, if you'll forgive the somewhat tasteless comparison, like a highly preventable virus in a vulnerable population. With each new wave of attention comes another wave of people who really, really need to talk to me about a subject I burnt out on years ago.

I still believe what I wrote. I'm glad it's out there in case other autistic people need to hear it—or in case a non-autistic person is at least willing to consider another perspective. I'm also genuinely dismayed that the connection between anti-vaccine conspiracy theories and anti-autistic prejudice is still an issue and that people are still suffering needlessly as a result of it. But I never want to fucking talk about it ever again. I don't want to engage in "friendly" debate. I don't want to write any more follow-up pieces. I never want to stumble through another awkward moment when someone brings me the latest news on vaccines and their lack of autism-causing germs with all of the good intent and all of the welcomeness of a cat bringing their owner a recently slaughtered bird. My efforts have made as much difference as they're ever going to in this realm.

Negative or positive, no one has had anything new to say to me about it in almost half a decade now. It's just this constant presence in the background of autistic life, buzzing like a particularly grating fluorescent light: People hate and fear the concept of you so much that the risk of disease and possible death is preferable to the risk of having to care for or about someone like you.

I don't regret—and I won't stop—seeking a bigger audience, either. I worked in complete obscurity for years. When I weigh the positives and negatives, writing in this slightly less marginal level of obscurity is still preferable to the alternative. Nor do I want people to stop responding to my work at all. For every comment that pierces me, there always seems to be another that truly humbles me. It takes a while to work through those emotions, too, but it means the world to me to feel like I've made a difference in someone else's existence. Even if I had other options—which, at this point, I really don't—I wouldn't trade writing for anything else. Unless pillow fighting somehow became a viable option again.

(If anyone wants to accuse me of attention-seeking or profiting off a very serious condition, well, you're half right. I do very, very earnestly want to help other autistic people. And writing is the only thing I'm good at, so this is really the only thing I can contribute to the cause. But I am only human, and there is a part of me that thinks that, if my own autism has had a negative impact on my ability to grow my writing career, then I should at least be able to make back some of my lost opportunities and wages writing about it.)

Being a writer and everything that comes with it does add another layer of difficulty to the challenges of surviving in the confounding world of normal people, though. It's a further drain on the energy I need for those tasks, too. So it's especially frustrating when my already depleted resources are once again diverted to something that never should have involved me to begin with.

I'd still choose autism over measles. (My father, who has first-hand experience with both, is also Team Autism, by the way.) But I'd be inclined to consider measles over needing to have this conversation at all.

STEP TWELVE

Burn out and watch 105 episodes
of a 50-year-old TV show

I WAS BURNT-OUT BEFORE IT WAS COOL.

I'm sorry. I try hard to curb my worst smug hipster impulses, which is no small task for a pedantic former music journalist with black plastic–framed glasses and a penchant for becoming obsessed with obscure things that inexplicably go on to attract mainstream attention. But it's true, and I'm still bitter about it. So I'm going to indulge my need to assert my saddest of all bragging rights: I was tired and broken back when all of the normal people who are now talking about their own cases of millennial burnout were still calling it being lazy and making excuses.

I called it autistic burnout, a term I learned not from professionals but from my fellow autistics trying to illuminate the gaps in the autistic experience that the so-called experts on us were either missing or ignoring. It describes a fairly common phenomenon that autistic adults were noticing in their lives. When faced with periods of major change, we can see a sizeable shift in our autistic traits. Causes of autistic burnout can include forcing yourself to pass as neurotypical, major stress or upheaval, sensory or emotional overload and illness. Symptoms can include a decrease in motivation, loss of executive function, selective mutism, problems maintaining social skills, memory loss, lethargy and decreased tolerance for sensory or emotional sensitivity. Basically, we hit a point where we can no longer manage our issues or keep up appearances in the same way that we have been and we end up feeling and/or looking "more autistic" as a result.

I'd been lurking on the periphery of autistic burnout for years, shaking off mild periods of confusion and exhaustion like a fighter moderately rocked by a strike. In the spring of 2015, I got knocked the fuck out. In my case, I think it was just a culmination of my entire life up until that point. Digging out from the catastrophic meltdown that had forced my diagnosis was very much a two steps forward, one and five-sixths steps back scenario. I was making progress, but I was *tired*. At least subconsciously, I was starting to realize that some of the coping mechanisms I was currently employing might not be long-term solutions.

My attempt to have a normal career in fitness, for example, was verging on unfeasible. Confirming that I was autistic allowed me to step back and re-evaluate what was possible and what was actually interesting to me in that line of work. I was able to give myself permission to drop some aspects of the gig that I was probably never going to become any better at or come close to enjoying, like teaching spinning to entitled rich people who refused to remove their sunglasses during class but then left complaints about my eye contact at the front desk afterwards. This gave me the time and energy to discover my own niche—private clients with mental health issues who felt alienated by bootstrappy mainstream gym culture—and develop that. I was a decent trainer once I found my element, but even that became disproportionately draining after a while. My issues with processing empathy meant that I was absorbing all of my clients' emotions and carrying them around with me almost constantly.

The amount of travel involved in going to and from homes and gyms was overwhelming, too. Those pre-session panic attacks on public transit became a part of my regular routine.[65] Then I stopped being able to sleep at all in anticipation of the next day's slate. All of the studying I'd done on heart rate training at least came in handy when I needed to identify how far out of a healthy resting zone my anxious ticker was racing.

The modest amount of freelance writing on pop culture, and now autism, that I was keeping up on the side was more fulfilling, but also more fraught. The version of *Chart* that I knew, loved and wrote for shut down in 2011, and I was given an opportunity at *Spinner/AOL Music*. When they ceased operations in 2013, I was able to pivot to *Huffington Post Music Canada* and pick up some assignments for *Vice*'s music and mixed martial arts sites. *HuffPo Music* closed shortly after. *Fightland*, the MMA sub-section, was running on fumes and was quietly swallowed up by *Vice*.[66] Constantly leaping from one great and hard-working but ultimately doomed outlet to the next—and trying to manage the grief, survivor's guilt and fear for the future that came with each closure—was not an ideal situation for someone who struggles with change and emotional regulation.

Switching between these two drastically different jobs was getting harder for me, too. I'd read that making and adapting

....

65 There's a reason why I used transit-based anxiety in my measles op-ed earlier that year as a specific example of how I was struggling. Toronto's infamous TTC is an overcrowded, passive aggressive, sensory carpet-bombing hellhole and only half of its unwritten rules make sense, if someone deigns to explain them to you. I spent every minute of my transit time hyper-alert to any offence or inconvenience I might be causing others and trying to choke down my reactions to unrelenting waves of sounds, lights, smells and unavoidable body contact. *And* nervous about the next session and trying to recover from the emotional and cognitive toll of the previous one. Which meant that I was spending hours a day with a racing heart, shaking hands and chest pains.
66 Bless its weird little heart, *Fightland* managed to hold on until 2017.

to transitions—everything from simple, regular shifts like bedtime to major life changes like puberty—can be more challenging for autistic people. But I never really appreciated how true that was for me until I had to switch gears from writing an eight-hundred-word profile with multiple sources to planning a one-hour Pilates session for a client with kyphosis, painfully tight hip flexors and limited shoulder mobility over the course of an afternoon. Or run straight from an indoor cycling class for a small group with varying goals and experience levels to reviewing a Lady Gaga concert. My brain was getting foggier and my nerves shorter with each about-face.

My life outside of work was going through its own pushes and pulls. Therapy was effective, but slow. I wasn't just unlearning my coping mechanisms, I was trying to repair the damage they'd done. Everything that I'd spent the past three decades doing to survive was starting to catch up with me. Trying not to look autistic had consumed my time and energy, and left me with little to contribute to the areas that actually meant something to me, like my family, my friends and my work. And the maintenance of those aspects of my relationships—dinners, drinks, emails, family events, heart-to-hearts, just checking ins, phone calls, movie nights, texts and everything else that goes into caring about someone else and sharing in their highs and lows—as much as I cherished them, was also getting harder for me.

I don't recall exactly how it all spiralled (even more) out of control, which might be the most telling symptom of all. Despite being a person who can recount mistakes that I made when I was three in great, anguished detail, I cannot say exactly how I started screwing this one up so badly. I remember being exhausted, although that couldn't have been anything new. I noticed that I was starting to make more typos and other small errors in my written work, which truly horrified me, because I'd always taken pride in how clean my copy was. I thought my borderline anal perfectionism in this regard was one of the better side-effects of my brand of autism.

There was also a three-month war with my sock collection where I simply couldn't find the right consistency to please my feet. It was yet another pathetic recreation of "The Princess and the Pea." I liked a certain amount of fuzz against my skin and a certain amount of a buffer between me and my shoes, but felt physically repulsed anytime that fuzz started to pill and rub against my feet in an imbalanced way. So I'd spend a good fifteen to twenty minutes each night meticulously performing surgery on my socks, trying to remove the latest batch of offending nubs. My ability to filter out other sensory issues was less tragicomic, but was becoming almost as grinding. I had to put my phone on vibrate because text message notifications became too much for me to handle. Then I broke our TV remote because I couldn't handle the sound of the vibrations. (Sometimes so-called "high-functioning" autism means having just enough clarity of mind to stop yourself from smashing the expensive offending item and throwing something that seems more expendable instead.)

In general, I felt like I was slipping somehow. I started making a lot of nervous *Flowers for Algernon* jokes when trying to describe my predicament to others, but they weren't entirely jokes. A part of me was worried that all of the headway I'd made since childhood was about to disappear. Even if the work involved with keeping up those efforts was breaking me, I was terrified of losing all that I'd gained with them.

Somehow I maintained enough self-awareness to understand that this low-grade disaster couldn't continue and that I was going to have to make some changes—and somehow I managed to scrounge up just enough self-motivation to try. The first thing I did was reach out to sympathetic family and friends and warn them that I was going through a rough patch and probably wouldn't be the most reliable— or pleasant—person for the next while. Then I spent some time trying to figure out how to express my gratitude for their offers of help while politely passing on it, a series of actions that required even more of my diminished emotional reserves. (This is the mixed blessing of having normal people who truly love you but don't entirely understand the parts of you that you haven't figured out how to explain to them yet. With no better information on how to help you, they will offer what makes them feel better. And you're left rejecting so many touching but useless acts of grace. So many people I care about wanted to take me out for drinks, and coffees, and chats. I just wanted those offers to still be on the table—and to be worthy of them—when I figured out how to leave my bed.) I also cancelled or rescheduled any work that I could.

The hard part, though, was figuring out what the hell I could actually change. I kept reflexively making that damned eye-ish contact, regardless of how unpleasant it could feel, long after I'd officially given myself permission to stop consciously forcing the issue. I quit policing my stimming, but kept instinctually gravitating toward what I considered more socially acceptable repetitive movements, like playing with my hair in public instead of flapping my hands.

My only hope came from a most unlikely and seemingly superficial source: the first few episodes of *The Man from U.N.C.L.E.* The 1960s spy satire was an old love of mine, dating back to my bedroom hermit phase, when YTV used to air it at one a.m. I'd spent years obsessed with its playful tone and its sardonic, floppy-haired Russian, and was starting to feel a bit possessive of the series as the premiere of the Guy Ritchie reboot crept closer. Somewhere in the middle of convincing one of my remaining editors that I was the only person truly qualified to review the film for them, I had declared that I would rewatch all 105 episodes of the original series in order to prepare for this most important of missions.

I had just begun this massive undertaking when the brunt of the burnout hit me. Initially, it felt as depleting and empty as almost everything else did at the time. Once the show began to hit its stride around the third episode, though, I was reminded of why I'd enjoyed it so much. Soon after that, I felt the first pangs of the old obsession returning like all of Celine Dion's memories coming back to her now in the chorus of a power ballad.

With no other viable options for my healthy de-normalization project on the horizon, I thought, *Fuck it. Let's do this.*

During my first *U.N.C.L.E.* phase, I had thought of my intense fixation on the show as the result of me being weird and having no life. I wasn't that off base, but I now understood that there was a little more to it than that. It was a "special interest," a term used to describe the act of an autistic person getting really into their shit, to put it in clinical terms. Professionals who work with the autistic population tend to describe this behaviour as a detriment. To them, it's an all-encompassing preoccupation, or an abnormally intense area of focus. Left unchecked, these obsessions could risk taking over our lives entirely. Autistic people tend to see the situation differently. To us, these interests can be a source of incredible joy, and a refuge from the unrelenting stress of the outside world.

Mine always seemed to show up when I desperately needed some sort of break from whatever else was going on in my life. The *Titanic* came to me when I was first starting to realize that I was different from other kids. David Lynch's *Dune* film surfaced when those other kids started to figure it out, too. Indie rock and *The Man from U.N.C.L.E.* were there for me when I bottomed out of school and started the lonely rebuilding process. Wrestling took over when I took my first nervous steps back into the outside world and adulthood.

Shame had snuck in not long after *Dune*, though. Very early on, I'd learned that loving things this way, especially the kind of things I loved, was not appreciated by other people. My intense excitement was uncool, embarrassing, off-putting, boring, annoying and/or not becoming of a young lady. And my expressions of it were tolerated by only my most indulgent loved ones. So I learned to hide it. Or, more accurately, I learned that I should hide it, desperately tried to, and then reproached the piss out of myself every time I failed to do so.

With a second wave of *U.N.C.L.E.* hyper-fixation on the horizon, I weighed how much these interests seemed to give me against how much I'd sunk into trying to spare other people from me while I was in the throes of them, and decided to do a little experiment. I would just let this thing run its course. I wouldn't keep tabs on how much time I was sinking into it, or worry that I'd gone too far. Nor would I meticulously monitor how often I was talking about it in casual conversation, or posting about it on social media. There would be no holding back, no angst about how weird I must seem to other people, and absolutely no trying to anticipate their reactions and trying to shrink to suit what I thought they would want from me. If anyone got bored of me, if they muted me or deleted me, or wanted to stop talking to me entirely, then let them. As long as the obsession remained at least relatively healthy for me and respectful of others—i.e., as long as it didn't interfere with my life or my most important relationships, and as long as I wasn't, say, showing up at a funeral and insisting on talking about a half-century-old TV show the entire time—I was just going to be my intense, dorky, overly invested autistic self and see how that worked out for me.

This probably sounds inordinately self-indulgent and inconsequential to anyone who has come here looking for serious insights on all things autism. To be perfectly fair, it kind of felt that way to me at the time. It was, however, the best that my even-more-broken-than-usual brain could come up with and all that my even-more-broken-than-usual everything could handle. But this isn't a story about how to rebuild from or stave off one of the most serious threats facing a large swath of the autistic adult population. This is just a little anecdote about how one autistic adult started to notice how much of her life she was wasting on ultimately useless efforts.

I didn't expect much to come from my glorified binge watch. My idle hypothesis for this half-assed experiment was that the benefits would be in line with any staycation. I'd get some mental and physical rest, have some fun geeking over something I loved and achieve a base level of restoration. So I was surprised at how much better I felt, and how quickly I got there.

My first indication as to why that might be came fairly early in the process, shortly after viewing "The Shark Affair" (season 1, episode 4). An exchange between the two main characters had made me finally start to see why Napoleon Solo/Illya Kuryakin slash fanfiction[67] predated Kirk/Spock. Despite being a massive fan of homoeroticism in general, I'd always rejected the pairing, because I didn't think Napoleon was good enough for Illya (and because I thought the dreamy, sarcastic Russian should become a real boy and marry me). Now I was beginning to question myself, and wanted to share this potentially groundbreaking revelation with the world. I was home alone, so I took to Facebook to make the announcement.

....
67 Slash is homoerotic fanfiction. And the subject matter of my aforementioned novella, which I still think someone should publish.

I took a screen cap, wrote a few silly lines about how the spies appeared to be drinking, flirting and getting their suits mussed up in their boss's office, and how this threatened to shift my entire worldview ... and then I hesitated. I rewrote it, deleted the rewrite, and then rewrote it again and threw a giant apologetic disclaimer at the top. Further tinkering, overthinking and general consternation ensued. It wasn't until I reminded myself that I was on the verge of sabotaging a very pressing experiment that I was able to produce an approximation of my original vision, take a few deep breaths and post.

In total, the process must have taken almost twenty minutes and immeasurable unnecessary stress. All for something that would take my friends, most of whom knew full well I was a massive nerd with a soft spot for homoerotica, three seconds to scroll past if they didn't care for it. I could have gone for a walk in that time. Attempted a nap. Watched a chunk of the next episode. But I spent it neurotically curating myself for people who already knew I was weird, and were apparently good enough with that to remain virtually connected with me in some way.

Further viewing and fixating chipped away at that initial self-consciousness, and I was soon sharing my enthusiasms, reflections and tangential deep dives with a shameless ease. I researched tie-ins and parodies, scoured fanfiction archives and read up on the history of the original *U.N.C.L.E.* fans and the important role they played in fandom as we now know it. I developed a number of long-winded and wide-ranging theories on the show and its cultural significance (and its gayness) and shared them on social media and with anyone who cared to listen. Then I posted some more. Then I posted even more.

The extent of my gleeful perseveration during this period cannot be overstated. A few weeks in, a friend who had always seemed amused by my obsessions bemusedly commented on one my latest social media missives. "I just counted and this is the twenty-sixth post you've done in a row in what I am now calling The U.N.C.L.E.-ing," wrote this friend, who I promised not to name in my book after he admitted that he was feeling a little guilty about his actions. "This is extreme, even for you." I drew a line on a piece of paper and marked the farthest point on the left "When I started." The other end was "When I've gone too far." About a fifth of the way from the left, I drew a dot and labelled it "When [friend who shares a name with the pro wrestling promotion founded by Mitsuharu Misawa] says I've gone too far." Then I took a photo of it, sent it to him and dreamed up another post.

Not all of my unfettered digressions were illuminating or entirely sensible during The U.N.C.L.E.-ing. Consuming 105 episodes of anything in a matter of weeks is going to melt your brain a little, and that goes double if the third season involves Robert Vaughn dancing with a man in a gorilla costume, and the turgid fourth season makes you retroactively miss that moment. A few of my better notions sharpened into proper ideas, though, and the best of those became pitches. With the aid of my freshly cultivated shameless streak and general lack of any ties to reality, I sent them out. I actually worked up the nerve to cold pitch a dream publication. Successfully.

When *The A.V. Club* published my giddy treatise on the groundbreaking sexual appeal of Illya Kuryakin, the importance of respecting your female fanbase and the timeless beauty of Illya's iconic hair, something even more improbable and wonderful happened: other, almost equally overinvested fans reached out to me. Unabashed *U.N.C.L.E.* discussion naturally gave way to more general bonding, and I went from thinking that my obsession might cost me real-life friendships to forging new ones as a result of it.

Approximately five weeks, 105 episodes, one regrettable TV reunion movie, three paying writing assignments, a net gain of two friends and one tattoo of Illya's badge to commemorate the occasion later, I concluded my experiment. Here are some of the things I learned and observed from it:

- The line between normal, healthy interests and weird and obsessive ones isn't always clear and is at least partially determined by the zeitgeist. Toward the tail end of The U.N.C.L.E.-ing, a trailer for *Star Wars: The Force Awakens* dropped and I watched a bunch of average geeks immediately go to town on it in a way that threatened to surpass anything I'd done in the throes of my spy obsession. When I voiced my annoyance at this disparity to a friend who was a long-time *Star Wars* fan, he simply said, "Now you know how I felt about sports in high school."
- Illya and Napoleon are soulmates.
- I had grossly underestimated how much time and energy I was still putting into trying to make myself palatable to other people.
- I had grossly underestimated how much that process was taking out of me. Within a week of that first *U.N.C.L.E.* epiphany post, I was more alert and my thought process was clearing up. My body and disposition felt lighter. And it wasn't just the kind of rest and relaxation you'd expect from taking a bunch of time off to chill in front of a TV, either. I felt less depleted, which was something I'd kind of assumed was no longer possible for me.
- Everyone had diarrhea on the set of *The Magnificent Seven*. (I read Robert Vaughn's memoirs as part of greater *U.N.C.L.E.* research. He brought it up there. Twice.)
- There really is someone out there for everyone. I made really good friends. Because they read my love letter to a fictional Russian spy I had crushed on as a lonely teenager.

Which was published in an outlet that I loved. And they reached out to me.

· All of the time, energy and life force I'd been sinking into holding myself back was far better spent on working on projects I cared about and hanging out with people who liked me just as I was.

· There was a slight possibility that I had grossly overestimated how much about me was not palatable to other people.

· Or that I had at least grossly overestimated how much of me was not palatable for people who had, for whatever unfathomable reason, decided they already liked me.

· It was also possible that I completely misunderstood which parts of me might be the real problem.

It was such a positive experience that I was almost grateful to Guy Ritchie for making a cinematic reboot of a half-century-old TV show that only the most arcane nerds still cared about in 2015. He completely butchered it, of course, and *The Man from U.N.C.L.E.* was added to the list of obscure things I love that inexplicably attract mainstream attention and suddenly aren't "mine" anymore. But none of this would have happened if he hadn't made the movie. I begrudgingly thank him for it. And beg him to resist all urges to make that lightly rumoured sequel.

My semi-indulgent downtime adventure was not a drastic fix, or even close to a permanent one. There are still an assload of pressing concerns that I am not doing the best job of addressing. I'm always tired and/or confused about something! I still burn out all over the place! But I'm actually glad my experiment ended up being so simple. If I'd wound up tackling a more pressing or grave aspect of my life, I might never have recognized just how much the relatively cosmetic bullshit was taking out of me.

The focus of my exercise might have been narrow, but the perspective it gave me wasn't. I didn't come away thinking "I fixed myself with TV, lol, autism is easy," or "The bad normal people are bringing me down and I should get to do whatever I want, whenever I want!" I thought, "If this one tiny action made such a viscerally recognizable difference in my life, what other unnecessary drains on my limited and not entirely renewable resources am I missing?"

The U.N.C.L.E.-ing forced me to further evaluate what I've been trying to do to exist in the world and how that's working out for me. Because I'm still working on the whole accepting-that-I-have-inherent-worth-as-a-human thing, I also felt compelled to break down how that was working out for the world.

I scoured my extensive efforts to become an alleged Participating Member of Society for energy inefficiencies like you might inspect a drafty house: Was I actually any good at trying to anticipate what's expected or demanded of me as an alleged Member of Society? If the aforementioned twenty minutes of tense hand-wringing over whether or not I should burden my Facebook friends with a silly post about Naps and Illya getting it on in Waverly's office was any indication ... not so much.

Was I just assuming that everything is wrong, panicking, overcorrecting and killing myself for no reason? Not necessarily. I hadn't imagined or overblown the serious pressures on autistic people to perform in certain ways or the consequences of falling short of those expectations. It was just that, in addition to addressing those vital real-world concerns, I had also managed to wildly overcompensate for faults that I was either misunderstanding or brutally overestimating. In elementary school, I once forgot to put my name on a test and my teacher asked me to write it out ten times in punishment. I was *mortified*. Clearly, she had not understood the extent of my mistake, or how much I should suffer for slipping. So I wrote the ten. Then ten more. Then another ten. I kept going until the teacher had to pull the "Sarah Kurchak"-sodden paper out of my hands in horror. It wasn't until my little audit that I realized this might not be a cute story.

When I moved to Toronto, I started listening to any footsteps that I heard behind me, trying to assess their rhythm and location. This wasn't for my safety; it was for their convenience. I would either match the rhythm and stay a polite, impediment-free distance in front of the owner of the footsteps, or try to reposition myself in relation to them to allow this person to pass me without any unwitting interference on my part. I was utterly merciless with myself if I slipped and a complete stranger with no more rights to sidewalk space and expediency than any other person using public infrastructure was inconvenienced by my existence for a second. It wasn't until this audit that I realized sonar pedestrian accommodation[68] is not a thing that anyone else does or expects. Exactly how much was I sacrificing for this place I thought I needed to secure in society? What was society getting out of my prohibitively expensive contributions? As far as I could tell, I had sacrificed most of my mental health and a touch of my physical health on the altar of society. All that society was getting out of it was one chronically anxious and depressed half person who had overthought everything from liking TV shows to being on a sidewalk.

What benefits might I hope to see in return? I am alive and am at least able to wander around in the world without much prejudice or persecution, which is a privilege afforded to far too few people. But there's little to no meaningful exchange between the individual and society when I'm living like this. Effectively ruining oneself just to provide absence

....
68 As opposed to basic awareness of other people and manners.

of annoyance or inconvenience to others in exchange for their allowance of your continued basic existence is not an optimal outcome for anyone involved.

As relatively frivolous as The U.N.C.L.E.-ing was, it's also had a substantial influence on how I think about some of the bigger and more serious issues in the autism universe. There's nothing like having your relatively privileged autistic life with its low level of support needs and solid base of family and friends undergo a viscerally recognizable transformation over an arguably insipid and inconsequential experiment to make you wonder what other unexplored or underestimated life-changing alterations might be possible for all autistic people. And make you further question what is expected of autistic people and who those expectations truly serve.

I'm not against any therapy or treatment that helps an autistic individual better cope with any sensory and social concerns they might have, and helps them navigate any of number things that might not make much instinctual sense to them, but I believe those skills should be nurtured in a way that is healthy for that individual and done for purposes that suit them.

Far too many mainstream solutions prioritize non-autistic whims over autistic needs. Why is eye contact still forced when so many autistic people have pointed out that the effort and discomfort involved actually makes us less capable of participating in conversations? Because it makes the normals *feel* like you're paying attention to them. Why is trying to force speech such an all-important task when many non-verbal autistic people can thrive using augmentative and alternative communication?[69] Because non-autistic

....

69 AAC (augmentative and alternative communication) is an umbrella term for methods that are used to substitute for and/or supplement speech and/or writing for people who have communication disabilities.

people prefer verbal communication.[70] Whether the problem
is that we don't talk at all or that we don't talk in exactly the
right way, the intervention seems to ignore what is viable for
autistic people in order to cater to what is comfortable for
everyone else.

The ideology upsets me as an autistic person who has
some understanding of the deep costs involved in meeting
non-autistic people's arbitrary standards of acceptability.
But it also confuses me as someone who cares about other
people. I wouldn't expect another person to fundamentally
alter or conceal almost every aspect of themselves and put
their well-being at risk just to earn my tolerance. I wouldn't
dismiss someone as a tragedy or burden if they couldn't, for
whatever reason, make those changes. Human interactions
that don't involve a degree of mutual exchange and common
ground sound kind of hollow and dickish to me. And way
more clueless, selfish, solipsistic, antisocial and potentially
boring than subjecting someone to a few ardent digressions
about that spy show/shipwreck/polarizing Lynch film with
the cool colouring book/gluteal-fixated pro wrestling promotion you're really into could ever be.

----

70 There's an entire industry dedicated to figuring out what pets are saying and
what they need, but few verbal people are willing to put in a fraction of that effort
to understand the non-verbal communication of their fellow human beings.

STEP THIRTEEN

Flail

IN 1988, MY FAVOURITE POWER POP BAND, THE POSIES, RELEASED their debut album. Young and equally filled with promise and piss-taking, they called it *Failure*. Ten years later—and two years after one too-clever-for-her-own-good teenager fell in love and overidentification with their sugary sweet harmonies and canker sore–tongued lyrics—they released what was intended to be their last album. In a similarly ironic spirit, they called that one *Success*.

The title always stung a little. Self-deprecatingly naming your swan song after your failed potential was one of the most Posies moves possible, but the Platonic ideal of the gesture couldn't entirely erase how unfair it all felt to me. Their only crime seemed to be writing jangly melodies and bitterly clever lyrics at a time when CD-buying consumers who were not me preferred their innermost feelings projected with fuzz and blunt angst. They had deserved to experience that word in earnest. However, as I've grown from sarcastic but still idealistic indie nerd with her whole life ahead of her to burnt-out freelancer making moderate gains in the field of keeping my head above water, I've really come to appreciate it.

I like to put *Success* on when I'm puttering around my apartment or trudging through my latest assignment. During my intermittent expeditions into the outside world, I used to blast it on my dying iPod, which I refused to upgrade,[71] until its clickwheel stopped responding to my touch. It's nice to have a soundtrack for the moment you realize that sometimes the concept of success wilts from prophecy to punchline.

When I was young, my upward trajectory was almost universally assumed. Not even my bullies thought to question this seeming inevitability. I was smart. I worked hard. I excelled at everything I tried, except gym and making friends. As long as I didn't want to be an Olympian or prom queen, I would continue to do well at anything I applied myself to. A rewarding personal life would just show up somewhere along the way, apparently.

My future was such a foregone conclusion that family, teachers and random friendly acquaintances informed of my plight all used it to comfort me at my lowest moments. Someday I'd show everyone. Someday I'd make it. And those girls would regret ever hurting me when I was famous/popular/rich/happy. Because I desperately needed to believe there was something better out there for me, because it appealed to the fragile ego I'd bandaged over the gaping hole where my self-esteem should be, and because I'd yet to face any perspective-growing non-social challenges in my short life, I completely bought into the idea too.

How did that work out for me? Well, I share a pleasant one-bedroom apartment with my ideal partner, an adoring cat and a stuffed dinosaur (in a building that will soon be

....
71 You know those stories about autistic children who will only wear a specific piece of clothing, or use a specific item, and the troubles they face when those things wear out and/or are discontinued? That's me and my black sixth-generation 80GB iPod Classic.

demolished to make way for condos). I'm currently able to support myself by doing meaningful, interesting work in my lifelong dream job (though opportunities are drying up and outlets are dying at an exponential pace). The uncertainty of my future buzzes like a fluorescent light in the background of everything I do (but maybe the world will end soon and none of this matters, anyway).

I don't leave home that much. Sometimes I think about all of the social demands involved in being in public and decide I'm not up to the task. Sometimes I choose to stay put because going outside doesn't entirely deserve its good reputation. Occasionally I intend to, but I get caught up in a random task or distraction and my immense capacity for inertia kicks in. I watch a lot of wrestling ... and more Ingmar Bergman.

It's a little like being stuck in my teenage bedroom again, down to the same *Dead Ringers* poster hanging on the wall, except now I have friends who will meet me when I'm ready to venture out in the world, or come to me when I'm in my hermitage. They text instead of calling, which is an infinitely less wretched and stress-inducing form of communication for me. And instead of having my whole life ahead of me, I'm running out of time.

I'm bubble-wrapped in love and support with few conditions, but my life is so fragile. I have no clue what's next and barely know what I'm doing now. I'm not truly proud of anything I've ever done. I'm not satisfied. I am displeased with myself in a way that exceeds the general self-loathing that seems to come with the job and is exhibited by my writing peers. How little I've accomplished weighs on me more with each wasted day and blown prospect.

I wouldn't say that I'm an abysmal failure or my existence is worthless. At least not outside of the throes of a proper autistic meltdown or a deadline-pushing episode of writer's block. But I am not living the life that was misguidedly prophesied to me or expected of me. I've yet to meet my realistic contingency goals. Even when I petulantly declared that I was going to be a struggling, tortured writer when I grew up, during a patronizing career seminar in grade eight, I was picturing a little more than this.

There are a number of factors that contributed to my complete inability to realize any of the above. Some of them were in my control. I did choose to pursue a career in a completely unreliable industry. I couldn't have predicted the rate of its decay when I made that choice, but I did know that writing was a difficult and demanding job with a high failure rate. Others—like class, chance, an entire industry all but giving up on the written word because bad data told them to and the whole not-knowing-I-was-autistic-until-it-almost-killed-me thing—were a little more out of my hands.

There are also some grey areas I go back and forth on. Here's a dramatic recreation of how I try to process those factors when it's three a.m. again, my legs are twitching, my brain is grinding like a dying hard drive and my heart is thudding in my throat like I'm in an overwrought reimagining of "The Tell-Tale Heart" and the murder victim is my potential:

Maybe the problem is that you didn't have enough drive. Maybe you weren't truly motivated. But ... my constant exhaustion suggests that I was attempting to push myself to or past my limits. *Yeah, well, maybe you're just lazy. And have you ever considered that you've never produced anything of value that would merit the kind of writing career or life you wanted?* Constantly. But editors and fellow writers that I respect seem to think I have. *Yeah, well, maybe they just pity you. You're probably not good enough.* Or maybe it's all a fluke and my life could have just as easily been the fodder for an inspirational memoir about what can happen if you stay true to yourself and refuse to give up on your dreams, with a slightly different roll of the dice ... *No, there's no way that's it. You suck and you should probably just die.* Yeah, I suck and I should probably just die."[72]

I try not to dwell on the past to the full extent of my autistically fixated tendencies, but I do think about what might have been. I no longer resent that I slipped through the cracks in my childhood. I've talked to enough autistic adults who were diagnosed as children about the bullying, stigma and often traumatic interventions they received as a result to make me suspect that I'd only be differently broken and confused if anyone had picked up on the signs back then.

I do regret that I didn't know for sure earlier in my adulthood, though. Specifically, I wish that I had been armed with a diagnosis and more information before I got it into my head that it was time to grow up and get a real job. If I'd had a better awareness and acceptance of my limits, I don't think I'd have forced myself into so many situations that were never going to work for me. Perhaps I could have stopped beating myself up for failing at the parts of the job that were so brutally incompatible with my combination of neurology and personality a little earlier in the process. Maybe, if I'd had a better grasp of my strengths and weaknesses—and the potential explanations for them—I could have made better-informed decisions about my future.

I'm not talking about using my autism as an excuse to avoid challenges or letting my autism stop me from achieving things, or whatever other nonsense abled people start spewing when disabled people's choices and perspectives about their own lives aren't inspirational enough. I mean being able to apply an awareness of my autism—and, by extension, a greater awareness of myself—to my choices in life. Not to give up, but to figure out what I wanted and what was feasible for me, and to pursue that to the full extent of my abilities instead.

....

72 Negative self-talk has been condensed for length and relative clarity.

My wonky career path is a perfect example. Fitness was a job that I liked well in enough in a mildly stable field, but it presented challenges that I would never have been able to overcome without significant damage to my health, if at all. It involved an impractical timetable, prohibitive amounts of travel, an exhausting level of interpersonal interaction that was often intensely emotional in nature, and I never came away from a gig feeling like I'd done anything worthwhile for anyone. Media was an even less stable industry, but as I've mentioned, writing had been my dream job since I was in kindergarten. It provided flexible hours, fewer demands on my limited social reserves, people sometimes told me I didn't suck at it and I seemed to able to perform it without risking complete physical and mental collapse.

I'll always wish that I could have known and weighed all of the above and realized that the latter option was, bizarrely enough, the more responsible choice. I'll always wonder what could have happened if I had applied everything I invested in pursuit of a "real" future—the money, hours, health, self-loathing and desperate desire to improve at any cost—to something that was better suited to me and closer to what I really wanted out of life. Or how much more secure I might feel about any aspect of my life if I'd applied the same time, energy and obsessive dedication that I put into making myself more palatable to normal people into any other pursuit. Or if any of the above would have been easier to navigate if I could have grown up just a little less maladjusted. (Or how much better life might have been if I'd managed to parlay my time in the PFL into a career as a pro wrestling manager in a bizarre comedy wrestling promotion.)

I had no idea, though. Even when I suspected that I might be autistic, I didn't know what that really meant, either. So I made decisions that either seemed right to me at the time or felt like what I supposed to do. Now, depending on the sunniness of your outlook, I'm either in the early stages of rebuilding from those mistakes or suffering their consequences for the rest of my life.

This is probably the part where I should provide some tangible details about my current existence to keep my non-autistic writers engaged and any remaining voyeurs sated, but I honestly don't know what to tell you. I get up. I waste time on the internet. I text my mom, possibly about wrestling. I write something. I hate it. I waste time on the internet. If Aaron's at work, I might get a text asking if I've eaten lunch or gone outside yet today. I probably haven't. If he's home, food occasionally appears. I waste time on the internet. I watch wrestling. Sometimes I get motivated enough to exercise. I watch wrestling. I spend hours trying to fall asleep and not quite as many hours sleeping.

Days and weeks can blur together. I chart the months and years mostly by the various holes and funks I've blundered into and either crawled out of or been dragged out of by the unfailing efforts of my loved ones. I coasted on the U.N.C.L.E.-ing reprieve until a somewhat unexpected death in the family shattered me, and the loss of my childhood home unmoored me in 2016.[73] Then I could no longer process, compartmentalize or otherwise handle the American election. My own fear for the future was hard enough, but my wonky empathy soaking up everyone else's reactions, especially on social media, broke me. I spiralled further in the first half of 2017 thanks to a too-relevant-for-comfort resurgence of my quirky childhood nuclear holocaust phobia[74]

....

73 It's latent autistic grief, not stereotypical autistic coldness, that's keeping my descriptions of these gutting events so brief and clinical.

74 I have few complaints about my upbringing, but I do wish that my otherwise exemplary parents had not explained the plot of *Testament*, a 1983 drama that follows a San Francisco family as the world slowly falls apart in the wake of a nuclear holocaust, to me when I was four years old. I have never recovered from this early onset existential dread.

but rallied with the assistance of a pleasantly distracting summer vacation. Then 2018 was a bit of a slog and a mixed blessing—Aaron and I lost one beloved cat and gained another—but the wrestling-related parts were good. The parts of 2019 that didn't involve writing or editing this book were nice enough.

I've stumbled personally and professionally over the course of these years, and left a smattering of missed opportunities and unintentional hurt and disappointment in my wake. But I'm still here, which is a legitimate accomplishment for someone of my neurotype and age. I have people in my life who I adore and, despite my constant fears to the contrary, they assure me that the feeling is mutual. I am in good physical health outside of my disastrous sleep cycle and my likely anxiety-induced high resting heart rate. In a bad year, I still make at least twice the average for a Canadian writer,[75] but that's more of a damning portrait of a desperate industry than a success story. My basic financial and emotional needs are, for the time being, met.

And in between all of those valleys and crevasses, there has always been something worth hanging on for. I've strengthened my bonds with the people who have held on to me and, although I'll never feel like I can ever pay them back for their care and patience, none of them seem intent on keeping score. I've visited places and had experiences that once seemed impossibly out of reach to me. I've celebrated with my loved ones as they reached major milestones in their lives and, if you're reading this book, then I suppose I've achieved one of my own.

When I briefly dabbled in long-ish distance running in my late twenties, I picked up the habit of running toward

....
75 According to a report released by the Writers' Union of Canada in 2018, writers made an average of $9,380 in 2017. So no, this wasn't a humble brag.

a series of small landmarks along my route. It was a way of breaking daunting runs into physically and psychologically manageable chunks: Just make it to the stoplight. Just make it to that tree. Just make it to that mausoleum.[76]

When I'm low, which is often, I now apply the same motivational technique to my life: Just get to the next misadventure with Aaron. Keep going until the next visit home to my parents, and the next trip with Mom. Make it to the next publication date. Hold on for the next dinner/drinks/show with the *Chart* survivors/PFL women/other beloved weirdos I met through those initial beloved weirdos.

That uncertain future of mine lurks over everything, though. Now that I do know that I'm autistic and I do have a better grasp of what that entails, I have become more aware of some of the issues that I could start facing with age. My cognitive processing speed is starting to slow down a bit, which means that I'm not as able to mask and keep up with the normals as I used to be (and my patience has waned to the point where I'm less inclined to try). Older autistic people with uteruses have warned me that menopause can do a unique number on our kind, and that there are little to no medical resources to help us through that. I make more typos and lose words more often than I used to, which makes me worry about my future the way Robert Vaughn's sharpshooter character in *The Magnificent Seven*[77] worried about his deteriorating reflexes. If there comes a time when I can't write—when I can't communicate in the only manner that has ever made anything approaching sense to me—then I'm truly fucked. Based on this prose and essay structure, I'm

....

76 I mostly ran in cemeteries. They're relatively quiet. Their asphalt paths are more joint-friendly than concrete sidewalks. And I'm part goth.

77 Did you know that everyone had diarrhea on the set of *The Magnificent Seven*?

guessing some of you would be tempted to argue that it's already begun.[78]

I figure my best hope is to assemble a body of work good and odd enough to earn both money and some kind of eccentric genius status. If I can somehow manage that, I'm 99.3 percent sure that all of my foibles—autistic and otherwise—will be treated as the quirks that come along with the whole being strangely brilliant thing, as opposed to the detriments and deal breakers they are now. If that fails, there's always the possibility that the world will end before my issues spiral too far out of control.

Right now, though, I am mostly okay. A bit melancholy, confused and prone to frequent panic attacks that feel like a ceaseless scream lodged in my throat, but I have my good days. Plenty of neutral ones, too. I wake up each morning feeling wildly behind but not quite defeated yet. Which isn't the worst possible outcome for a lifelong depressive weirdo who, you know, spent almost three decades wandering around clueless about a key component of what made her who she was. I wouldn't call it optimal, though. At least I hope it's not.

I suppose there is one way in which I've realized a lifelong goal, albeit in a brutal monkey's paw kind of way.

When I was young and still imbued with a modicum of promise, I used to dream of becoming a role model of some sort. Not in the sense that I ever imagined myself to be

---

78 I've certainly wondered. Writing this chunk has become such a miserable and seemingly hopeless process that I described it as "like living in that horse-killing swamp from *The NeverEnding Story*" to Aaron. Who didn't get the reference. And then I cried because I had no other way to describe my struggle. And because I will never again feel the sense of possibility that I felt when I first watched the film as a child and thought you could literally live in a ceaseless story forever. I couldn't articulate that, either. As I write this footnote, I still have no idea how I'm going to land this damned thing. At least I nailed the title.

an admirable, upstanding citizen. I think I always knew that I'd be a bit of a peculiar outsider, perhaps a borderline miscreant. But I did imagine that I would write things that other people could appreciate, and do things that would make the next generation want to grow up to be like me in some way.

And now I get all of those parents telling me, "I wish my child were like you!" Or "If my child were like you, I would have nothing to complain about." Or "If my child were like you, I'd consider them cured." Or, for some ungodly reason, "I wish my child could write as well as you do."

Of course, these comments are rarely meant in earnest. Even if I hadn't been studying the bladed tones of sarcasm and irony while everyone else was partying, I'd be able to detect the sneers. For every person who sees a sliver of hope in my story, exponentially more see an unrealistically positive outcome. By standards I rarely understand, let alone agree with, they've determined that I have it better than any person with autism could ever hope for. This is usually attached to some implication that I should, therefore, just shut up and stop distracting people from the real problems related to autism. The real problems usually have something to do with how awful autism is, how burdensome autistic people are on their families and how the only thing that can stop this tragedy is finding a cure.

It hurts a little to have a sentiment you've ached to hear for so long lobbed at you in predominantly bad faith. "I wish my child could write as well as you" really gets under my skin because it's an insult to my experience and my work.[79] Autistic or not, most children don't write like me because I am an adult who has spent almost three times

---

79 Not to mention that "I wish you could write!" is one of the cruellest curses you could bestow upon a child. No fairytale villain ever stooped so low.

as long working on my one skill as they have been alive. I didn't write like this when I was their age, either. If the angry prose that's been hurled at me is any indication, their parents still can't.

But my wounded ego is a secondary concern. What truly bothers me about these comments is the sentiment that my life is as good as it could possibly get. That it's somehow selfish to want more for myself, and downright unrealistic to wish the same for anyone else. Or that it's a waste of attention and resources to demand—or actively work for—better lives for autistic people that also allow us to be who we are, as we are. Especially not when the alternative that most of my opponents seek is to funnel even more money into looking for the cause of autism—and for a cure.

Personally, I think it's unrealistic and irresponsible to put all of your hopes for a better future into this nebulous quest. I don't believe in a cure for autism. Not in the sense that I am ideologically opposed to it, but in the way that I don't believe in minotaurs. I simply can't fathom that there will ever be a magic pill or treatment that will eradicate something as complex as whatever it is that makes us tick differently. If experts have yet to figure out why we are how we are, or how to help us, how are they going to figure out how to eradicate us? Even if I thought we might see a cure for autism in our lifetimes, I can't imagine being content to wait for it. Nor can I stomach my outcome being treated as the absolute best any autistic person can hope for until this mythical neurological rapture comes along.

This is why I've started to embrace the idea of being a cautionary tale. My story isn't a lofty goal for any autistic human being unless you value appearance over substance. It's only a success story if you value arbitrary benchmarks over well-being. If I can't be the person I wanted to be—or the person anyone else wants to be[80]—I can at least be the kind of person I wish I'd had in my life. Someone not exactly like me, but close enough to get it. A soul who could share the wisdom (or "wisdom") of their experiences with me. Someone who could look at me and my choices from the perspective of our similarities and their history and say "Christ, kid. Don't be like me."

There's an addendum to that Posies story. They continued to play together after the release of *Success*. The shows were sporadic at first, but they were touring again just a few years later. They released a new album in 2005, and have produced two more since then. I may remain a little resentful that they are not the international superstars that they deserve to be— and that they never seem to play Toronto in their current form—but they're still doing what they care about, still producing work that matters to other people. They're still going.

I've been more and more drawn to these kinds of second acts lately. I'm genuinely heartened by stories where the process is just as important as the goal, if not more. I'm finding heroes in people who find value in their work more than its reception, and people who just keep going because that matters, and because what else are you gonna do, anyway. Like Tetsuya Naito, the fallen heir apparent to the New Japan Pro Wrestling throne who clawed back from failure and humiliation to become a beloved workhorse antihero with a heart of gold. Discussing his atypical career arc in a 2018 documentary for the Japanese public broadcaster NHK, Naito eschewed any flowery notions of how your dreams will come true if you don't give up. He doesn't like those ideas. But,

....
80 It's always "I wish my child was like you," never "I wish I was like you."

he added, if you don't give up, you can see the light. That's exactly the level of inspiration I can work with these days.[81]

I'll keep plugging away, doing the best I can for the people I love and the dream job that somehow became my only hope and see what happens. It's not like I have much in the way of other options, anyway. Even if I did, I think I'd choose this. Or this without the raging depressive and anxious episodes. If more comes of my efforts, that's great. If not, at least I can serve as a cautionary tale for the next generation of autistic people and their parents. You can have a moderate percentage of all of the advantages in the world, do everything you think you're being told to do, work your ass off and still end up being ... whatever it is I am. If even one child doesn't have to go through things the way I have, or someone feels a little less unseen because of something I've said, written or half-articulately tweeted in a fit of dismay, that's still a victory.

And if anyone wants to tell me that they wish their child was like me after that? Well, I want more for that kid, and for all of us. Aim higher. I'm still trying to.

....

81 However, I have become equally fond of another wrestler named Daisuke Sasaki, who once declared that "life is about giving up." Make of that what you will.

STEP FOURTEEN

Make slight progress by retracing the steps of a nameless Cold War spy trapped in a bizarre and remote prison

THE MORNING AFTER MY FRIEND RACHEL GOT MARRIED IN HER English hometown, the Canadian contingent of the wedding party started trading post-wedding UK vacation plans. It was the first time that most of us had ever been able to afford or justify a trip there, and we all seemed determined to visit as many geeky sites as possible. Harry Potter was a common influence. So was Jane Austen.

Even among fellow nerds, though, I hesitated to join in.

My mother and I were one sleep and a nine-hour train journey away from a three-night stay in The Village, the perversely charming penal colony where *The Prisoner*'s Number Six was trapped and tortured after resigning from his secret service job. In real life, the place is actually a genuinely charming resort town in North Wales called Portmeirion, but the distinction is trivial to fans of the 1967–68 cult hit. Portmeirion is well maintained and largely unchanged since *The Prisoner* was filmed there, and I was as desperate to visit as Number Six was to escape it. I fully expected to be overcome with wordless, sobbing joy the second we stepped into the town; the anticipation was making my heart thud even faster than my chronic anxiety usually does. But to the others, I simply muttered, "Mom and I are going to this weird little village in Wales where they shot this weird old show that I'm kind of obsessed with" before attempting to lob the conversation in another direction.

Almost exactly two years after I had my ostensibly life-changing epiphany about the detriments of suppressing special interests and the benefits of wholeheartedly embracing them instead, I was still struggling to apply its basic findings on an ongoing basis.

My motives were partially practical. I've adored *The Prisoner* for almost twenty years and I still don't know how to explain it with anything approaching efficacy. It's a show about a spy, known only as Number Six, who quits and then gets kidnapped and trapped in a cheery-looking penal colony known only as The Village. A revolving door of nefarious types who go by the designation Number Two drug and torture him in a series of convoluted efforts to make him confess the reason behind his resignation. Number Six thwarts them with varying degrees of success as he attempts to discover the identity of Number One and escape. There's an evil white ball that chases him around. My mother has been *terrified* of that thing since childhood.

The show is, depending on who you ask, a searing indictment of the surveillance state and unchecked progress, a paean to individualism, a haunting exploration of an individual's struggles with themselves, a fun psychedelic romp, a nightmarish psychedelic romp, a fascinating look into the psyche of its creator and star, Patrick McGoohan, or some combination of all of the above. It's simply easier to stick to the little that I know for certain: It is weird. It's half a century old. And I am definitely obsessed with it.

The content of the synopsis wasn't the only stumbling

block, though. There was also the matter of delivery. When even the *Diagnostic and Statistical Manual of Mental Disorders* has something to say about the way you love things—restricted interests that could be considered abnormally intense get their own listing as a diagnostic criterion[82]—it can take more than a couple of years to unlearn your fear of expressing any enthusiasm whatsoever.

Unlike most of the autism features and autism-related concerns that matter to me as an autistic person—and that I've attempted to highlight in this book—there actually are a lot of research and resources on special interests. Unfortunately, much of it appears to be grounded in the assumption that anything autistic people do is wrong and dysfunctional. So instead of building a knowledge base about what these intense enthusiasms are, what they mean to us and how to foster them as part of a healthy, rewarding life, we get a lot of studies trying to figure out why special interests are wrong and what to do about them. Many experts still advise parents to discourage their children's focus on a single topic. Organizations like the UK's National Autistic Society offer a more balanced view of the positive role that highly focused interests and attachments can play in our lives in their materials,[83] but still warn parents to watch out for signs the hobby might be developing into an obsession.

There have been some promising steps toward approaching special interests as a nuanced and valuable component of autistic life as opposed to a de facto detriment. Barry M. Prizant, Ph.D., has a largely heartening chapter about encouraging enthusiasms and using them as a point of connection

....

82 American Psychiatric Association, *Diagnostic and Statistical Manual of Mental Disorders* (DSM-5). American Psychiatric Association (2013).
83 National Autistic Society, "Obsessions, Repetitive Behaviour and Routines." See https://www.autism.org.uk/about/behaviour/obsessions-repetitive-routines.aspx.

in his 2015 book *Uniquely Human*. Autistic researchers and writers are also starting to gain more attention for their vital work on the topic. But we're still seeing headlines like "Special Interests Hinder Self-Control in Children with Autism,"[84] too. It's no wonder so many autistic nerds like me are on guard.

Logically, I understand the positive role that these pursuits play in my life and I'll defend the validity and necessity of so-called "special interests" with the (over)zealous fervour I usually save for shipwrecks and spies. I'm vehemently opposed to any ideology that recommends discouraging them in autistic children in an effort to make us appear "less autistic" and thus more palatable to neurotypical people. Or guiding kids toward areas of focus that might make them more employable in the future, as if an autistic person's curiosity is only valuable if it's profitable.

I believe special interests have the ability to bring a sense of order and control to a world that is often baffling to us. I appreciate the escapism they provide when things get too overwhelming. I love the sheer joy people take in them for their own sake—the rush of wonder, fascination and accomplishment that comes from hurtling down obscure rabbit holes and grabbing hold of every piece of information you can find about something you love.

But ... a part of me is still that nervous child desperately scrambling to figure out the exact moment at which my passions became too overbearing, too off-putting, too *me* for other people. Adults found my childhood fascinations with the *Titanic* and dinosaurs amusing and would quiz me about them, which helped bring me out of my shell at school and family events. When I came down with a potentially fatal

....

84   Hannah Furfaro, "Special Interests Hinder Self-Control in Children with Autism," *Spectrum*, (May 12, 2018). See https://www.spectrumnews.org/news/special-interests-hinder-self-control-children-autism/.

virus in the first grade, my classmates drew pictures of the *Titanic* on the get well cards they sent to the hospital. Two years later, the shipwreck was reshaped into an insult hurled at me when they decided they'd prefer me dead. When both my interests and I stopped being so cute, other people stopped indulging and sometimes turned cruel, which left me confused, self-flagellating and anticipating rejection with my every move.

Indie rock helped me survive my adolescence and find the *Chart* universe. But I also found it made me even less palatable to everyone outside of that circle. No one else, it seemed, wanted to hear about my work. No one wanted to hear about *me*. My ideals, then, about self-acceptance and self-awareness aren't always a match for my history when I try to open my mouth.

I first came to *The Prisoner* at the tail end of my initial wave of fandom for *The Man from U.N.C.L.E.* and *The Avengers*. Once I was hooked on those weird sixties spy shows, it only made sense to track down another pillar of the genre. When I finally got my hands on a box set of the series's seventeen episodes, I fell hard.

Where *U.N.C.L.E.* and *The Avengers* had been the cheeky, bubbly escapism I needed at a time when my world was shrinking faster than my self-esteem and my hope for the future, I already *was* Number Six: unmoored and angry, clinging to the shreds of whatever made me me in a world that didn't seem to want it. I might not have been a top-ranked spy imprisoned in a surreal seaside prison, but being an undiagnosed autistic wasn't all that different. I was trapped in a world full of people and rules that didn't make any sense, while everyone else seemed intent on breaking me down. (And it was possible that I, too, was my own worst enemy in the end.)

The Prisoner made me feel like I was less alone in the universe. It was there to remind me of who I was, for better and worse. It also wound up being a source of bonding with my fellow music writers, because a certain percentage of music nerds are also obsessed with the show. (Iron Maiden even wrote a song about it.)

So when I wrapped up my return to *U.N.C.L.E.*, it only made sense to keep going with *The Prisoner*, making no apologies to anyone. And when my friend Rachel told me to start planning for a wedding in England, I decided that adding Portmeirion to my itinerary would be the ultimate celebration of my newfound ethos and lust for atypical life.

I didn't even wait until we made it there to sob; I started tearing up the second I spotted its pastel flourishes peeking out of the lush green countryside from the train. In many ways, Portmeirion was perfect. It was everything I dreamt it would be. It was worth the decades of anticipation, the slightly fraught misadventures in semi-remote North Wales and every cent that I'd invested in it. Hell, it was worth most of the isolation and frustration that had made me the kind of person who would take to a show like *The Prisoner* and want to visit The Village at all.

I, on the other hand, was weird about it. Not just in the weird "dress up like Number Six and run around the grounds proclaiming 'I am not a number! I am a free man!'" way that I'd planned, although I certainly did that, too. Weird in the sense that I started hesitating when I talked about our visit. Weird in the sense that it took me a day and a half to work up the nerve to wear the white-piped Village-style blazer that I'd purchased for the trip because I was afraid of what people—who were also visiting a place that had an entire store filled with *Prisoner* merchandise, including the exact same blazers—might think of me. Weird in the sense that the first few drafts of this essay, which I wrote in a *Prisoner* notebook with a *Prisoner* pen gleefully purchased from that very store, were self-flagellating affairs about feeling like I didn't "accomplish enough" on the pilgrimage. I eventually realized that my adventure hadn't been a culmination of my new unabashed special interest so much as it was a reminder that I was still a work in progress. And then I beat myself up about that, too.

But one of the things that I love about special interests—or at least the way that I experience them—is how they tend to intensify just as you need them to. So as I was stoking my anxiety with concerns about how tedious and unproductive I was being on my dream vacation, eviscerating myself for not being over the need to make the things I love as palatable as possible, I was also starting to feel a familiar rush of excitement for Portmeirion itself. Every time I read something about the history of the village (with the aid of the various books on the topic that were available in every room and gift shop on the property), every time we discovered a new trail, curiosity or dog cemetery on the grounds, this oddball paradise became more *interesting*.

Four months later, when some friends asked me about Wales, I briefly considered deflecting. Minimizing how much I'd loved it. Instead, I told them about Portmeirion's founder, Clough Williams-Ellis, and how he'd assembled this place out of off-kilter convictions about architecture and the future of Welsh manors and salvaged pieces of buildings that he had collected across the UK. I mentioned that the front of the building we stayed in—which happened to be Number Two's residence on *The Prisoner*—began its life as a fireplace in Cheshire. I said how grateful I was that one unapologetic eccentric had created this place almost a hundred years ago, and that another eccentric genius had shown up to film a stylish philosophical fever dream there fifty years ago, so that misfits like me could find our way there today. My friends responded with an enthusiasm so pronounced that even I, a person who still constantly second-guesses her ability to read other people, knew it was genuine.

Which made me feel less shame and self-reproach the next time I developed a new interest.[85] Which made my engagement in it even more rewarding. Which made the next interest[86] even easier and more enthralling. Like everything else I've been attempting to repair or improve about my life since the diagnosis, I take at least one step backward for every two forward, but I've taken so many steps with my special interests that I've actually made progress. Which, in turn, leaves me with a little more fuel in the tank to tackle the next issue.

Far from isolating and spoiling me, "indulging" in my special interests has actually expanded my world and fostered new and deeper connections with other people. Mom and I returned to Portmeirion in 2019 out of a shared fondness for its history and trails and had all sorts of fascinating conversations with the staff and other guests—including one woman who used to watch Clough, as she called him, wander the grounds when she visited as a child.[87] I went on a pilgrimage to New York with friends to see many of our favourite wrestlers in action and earnestly bonded over how much we loved them over cheesecake afterwards. Now I'm planning a trip to Japan for similar purposes.

I've also discovered that listening to each other info dump about our favourite things is a legitimate—and amazing—form of autistic communication. It doesn't matter if

....

85 In *Miami Vice*. What can I say? I'm a sucker for haunted authority figures in iconic blazers who are wrestling with themselves and their complicity in a broken system.

86 Wrestling. As you may have noticed already.

87 She told us an intriguingly macabre story about the property's previous owner. Apparently she died in the manor (now the main hotel) and the grounds had become so overgrown that people had to follow deer paths through the woods to find the structure and fish her out. Whether this account is real or apocryphal and possibly cribbed from *Sleeping Beauty*, listening to it was a magical way to spend an afternoon.

we know or care about the subject or not, we just love the enthusiasm. After lifetimes of being told that we don't know how to share properly, some of us are beginning to realize that maybe other people could learn a thing or two about listening. And that they're missing out.

All of which, I suppose, is my way of saying that there's this weird little village in Wales. One of my favourite shows was shot there. But that's only one of the reasons I'm kind of obsessed with it.

STEP FIFTEEN

Damned if I know

A THIRD OF THE WAY INTO THE PREMIERE EPISODE OF THE beloved working-class family cartoon *Bob's Burgers*, there's a *Rain Man* joke that almost justifies the existence of the 1988 film *Rain Man*.

Louise, the *enfant terrible* of the Belcher clan, calls her older sister autistic. The monotone-speaking, horse-obsessed, boundary-deficient Tina seems inclined to agree. While Bob is arguing with his daughters about their armchair diagnosis, clearly not for the first time, archetypical middle child Eugene tosses a handful of toothpicks on the ground and tells Tina to count them.

Tina, with a complete lack of conviction, guesses a hundred.

There are three.

Louise sighs in disgust and calls her the worst kind of autistic.

I had not yet seen *Rain Man* when I first watched this episode, but I sure felt like I had. It always seemed to show up when I was first researching autism to see if it might explain what the hell was going on with me. When a diagnosis confirmed that theory, people starting asking and teasing me about it. So I knew *Rain Man*'s plot, its characters and most of its hallmarks better than I knew most decent films that

I actually cared about. I was particularly familiar with the scene where Dustin Hoffman's autistic savant character, Raymond Babbitt, accurately assesses the number of matchsticks that a waitress drops at a restaurant because a friend had responded to my big autism news by asking me to count a pile of my own.

I got the Louise joke thanks to that. I appreciated the joke, though, because I'd often said the exact same thing about myself. I am not part of the 10 percent of the autistic population that classify as savants.[88] I can't count matchsticks, toothpicks or anything else to save my life. Aside from a brief run as a mathlete that I still can't explain, I am abysmal at anything involving numbers and shapes. My pain tolerance might be below normal—at least it felt that way when I was doing striking sports for fun. If you measure me against our most stubbornly prevalent stereotypes, I am the worst kind of autistic.

The closest thing I have to a special skill is politely laughing off the well-meaning but awkward *Rain Man* nods that people make when they don't know what else to say to me. Which has come in far handier than the average non-autistic person might assume.

I'm not sure I can properly describe the ridiculous and disproportionate presence that *Rain Man* has in many autistic people's lives. How do you begin to do justice to the absurdity of one thirty-year-old film—that wasn't written by, directed by or starring anyone like you, and that the real-life person it was based on didn't even have your neurology—having such a lingering influence on how people perceive you, talk about you and insult you? It wasn't until *The Good Doctor*, ABC's hit medical drama about an autistic savant Doogie Howser type,

---

88 And almost none of those savants, whose abilities and level of skill can vary greatly, are Rain Man, either.

premiered in 2017 that the zeitgeist's dependence on the film started to wane. (The fact that it took three decades for autism in pop culture to progress from a dreadful film about a white male autistic savant to a slightly less awful TV show about a white male autistic savant is another bonkers and beyond-description issue.)

I was six when *Rain Man* was released. I knew what being a rain man was before I was even aware of the word "autism," let alone the concept of it. Over the course of my life, it has been: a joke, an insult, a reason that I couldn't recognize myself and my presentation of autistic traits as autistic, a reason that no one else could recognize my traits and me as autistic, a source of more jokes and insults, a source of some of the most peskily enduring stereotypes about autism, a reference that everyone and their dog felt the need to make after I got diagnosed, a reason why everyone and their dog felt the need to ask me what my "special talent" was upon finding out I was autistic and an omnipresent reminder that people love autistic characters far more than they love autistic people.

Even if it had been an exemplary work of art, I think I would have grown weary of *Rain Man*. But the clips I'd seen and the essays I'd read on it made it look and sound cloying, treacly and more a parody of ways that Hollywood exploits disability than a film we should admire for its portrayal of it. Or for its portrayal of any humanity whatsoever, really. So I came to outright resent the film, its influence and the way it overshadowed any efforts that autistic people made to tell stories for ourselves. I bristled at any attempts to draw parallels between *Rain Man* and me and happily thwarted any tropes it perpetuated. "Being an autistic woman who is bad at math is bittersweet," I started quipping around that time. "You're sadly confirming one bullshit stereotype, but at least you're smashing another!"

And then I wound up misadventuring in Las Vegas with my closest blood relative.

For years, my kitsch-ridden heart had resisted the siren song of one of the world's most garish, absurd and unapologetic tourist traps. I was obsessed with Niagara Falls and going to Vegas felt a little like cheating on my true tacky love. The gambling aspect didn't appeal to me, because I couldn't stand the idea of being behind in debt or behind in any way. My dad played hockey with a guy who worked at Casino Niagara when it first opened, and I remember him coming home with stories about people mortgaging their homes and blowing the money on cards as a kid. These tales confused me even more than most human behaviour did. What could possibly be fun about risking so much? What happened to a person to make them unable to *stop*? Whatever it was, I didn't want any part of it. Hell, I didn't particularly feel like risking what little money I had on a vacation there at all.

Plus I really, really didn't want to invite any more *Rain Man* comparisons than I was already amassing.

In the dying months of my twenties, though, I stumbled into an all-expenses-paid junket to Sin City. Within five hours of landing, I had seen fake Egypt and fake Paris, witnessed the spontaneous combustion of a porn flyer dispenser, taken a free photo with a charismatic polar bear mascot at a three-storey Coke store, somehow gotten lost on The Strip (a destination named after its straight lined-ness), had a sobbing meltdown behind The Wynn's parking garage, acquired mild heatstroke and fallen completely in love. This ardour only intensified once the calamity wore off and the comped drinks kicked in.

I was so autistically smitten with Vegas that, almost as soon as I got home, I started figuring out how on earth I would be able to make it back again. And again. And again. I made a list of all the places I wanted to revisit and the foods I wanted to have repeatedly. I also started researching things I'd missed out on—places I'd noticed but hadn't had a chance to investigate, experiences and culinary delights I'd lost the nerve to try, etc.—and dreamed up ways to make good on all of them.

A little over a year later, I'd roped my mom into six nights and a 13.1-mile half-marathon event on The Strip. Within twelve hours of landing, we had discovered and reported the theft of my suitcase from the baggage carousel, both had a cry over it while trying to buy replacement clothes at the Fashion Show Mall, attended a free concert under Fremont Street's giant TV screen canopy, eaten entirely too much at a fancy buffet and then rushed to the Palazzo's washrooms so that I could puke most of it out. "Even with everything that has happened," Mom said as I was freshening up, "I think I love it here." This ardour only intensified once the calamity wore off and the lifetime-lasting memories kicked in.

Unless you want to draw a parallel between me crying over bras in a Dillard's and Dustin Hoffman's Kmart underwear freak-out scene, it was really nothing like *that movie*. There was no accurate counting of dropped objects or much in the way of gambling at all, let alone extraordinary house-beating blackjack. And I was, obviously, not a recent discovery to the woman who birthed and raised me. (We're quite close, having somehow gracefully transitioned from a mother and adolescent daughter who were frequently scolded for not cutting the cord to a mother and adult daughter who are often praised for how sweet our close relationship is. Although I assume we're still called weird, creepy and/or pathetic behind our backs.) There were no ulterior motives to our trip, either. We started going to events together when I was a lonely young music nerd who needed someone to go to concerts with and we both grew fond of the act of going places and doing things together. So even after I was old and friended enough to branch out on my own, we just ... kept it up. And no one learned any special lessons at the end of our visit to Vegas. Unless you count what I discovered about buffet overconsumption that one day.

You could argue that the amiable next-level compatibility I've developed with my favourite travel partner is merely the result of an overly permissive mother continuing to indulge her overgrown child. I myself have worried that our current relationship is little more than glorified Stockholm Syndrome when I'm feeling insecure, which is almost always. I am aware that a friendship with someone who lovingly reared and raised you can involve a level of comfort and leeway that friendships not quite so rooted in genetic and lifelong emotional ties can or should, and I'm eternally grateful for my luck in this regard. But I also believe that there is at least some level of mutuality in our adulthood adventures. She assures me that this is the case—the seven thousand times a day when I ask her if she's just humouring me/if there's something else or more she might prefer doing/if there's anything else I can do for her/if I can give her more money per day when we're on these trips. And I'm pretty sure the fact that she keeps suggesting new trips is a good sign that she wants to keep going on them.

Fuelled by that shared enthusiasm, we made Vegas an annual routine. I suppose a more cultured person might want to seek out new places year after year and expand their horizons a bit, but I'm really not that person. On account of the whole autism thing, I tend to like repetition and habit. Leaving my apartment to go to a destination I can navigate by heart to stay, eat and gawk at the same beloved places is plenty bold for me. I suppose a smarter or more self-preserving autistic might have sought this comforting dose of familiarity in a place that wasn't so visually, sonically and aurally assaulting or in constant flux, but I'd already fallen for that beautifully overwhelming and constantly self-reinventing trash heap. I was already in love with the patterns I'd formed there, and the sense of ease that came with going somewhere for neither the first nor last time. My anxiety and perfectionism put far too much pressure on me when I feel like I'm doing something for the only or last time. When I know that I don't have to do and see *everything*, when I know that I'll be back and can make up for anything I worry that I've missed out on or failed to appreciate properly, I can (almost) relax and enjoy what I am doing in that moment. In a way, I think it offers me something I long for in all areas of my life: the feeling that I have the time and the breathing room to take chances, make mistakes and try to make things right.

As Las Vegas established itself as an annual mother-daughter retreat, I somehow got it into my head that maybe I should just lean into the *Rain Man* parallels and try to learn how to count cards. I still wasn't much of a gambler. I'd grown fond of penny slots and a kitschy horse-racing game called Sigma Derby, but I was in it for the low-key trashy thrill of playing, not the hope of winning. I continued to feel no desire to risk much and no compulsion to chase my losses. The closest I came to using any math or strategy skills at all in casinos was the loose Gambling Losses vs. How Much I Would Have Spent to Buy the Comped Drinks I Received While Losing That Money tally I kept in the back of my head. As long as I was close to even, I was happy.

But I was starting to wonder. How *would* my autism fare at blackjack if I applied myself? This curiosity only increased when Ben Affleck was caught counting cards at the Hard Rock Casino. "If Ben Affleck can do it, surely you can!" I told myself. "And, well, if you can't pick up a skill that *Ben Affleck* can do, then maybe you can turn your hilarious failure into a stereotype-breaking teachable moment! How's that for Autism Awareness?"

The Rain Woman Project, as I jokingly referred to it, started to go south very early on in the research process. While lurking on gambling message boards for insight, I stumbled onto a discussion of blackjack table manners. Without even trying, I'd managed to find yet another online outlet for my worst fears and instincts! Naturally, I flung myself down that rabbit hole.

What I found was overwhelming and intimidating. The biggest complaint in most of these discussions was that regular players found it rude when newbies would blithely sit down at the table in the middle of a shoe. A quick google helped me figure out what a "shoe" was (it's the thing that holds the decks of cards on a blackjack table). But I couldn't find any information on how to identify what the middle of one would look like to the uninitiated, how a person might notice it without awkwardly staring at a table full of people and potentially creeping them out *and* making the pit boss suspicious, or what you should do if you did recognize that it wasn't an appropriate time but did want to hang around until it was.

Apparently things only got more complicated once you did sit down at the table. Completely silent people were considered rude or a bit of a buzzkill by all but the most serious players, but overly chatty people were almost as derided. If you could figure out the level of casual conversation Goldilocks would choose, you still had to worry about messing up the entire hand—or the entire shoe—for everyone by making one wrong choice of your own. And that seemed to be the worst sin of all.

I spent months trying to piece together how I'd manage to navigate the proper beginning of a game, engage in a satisfactory level of camaraderie and keep track of the acceptable moves that I should be making in my own game so as not to upset anyone else's, let alone keep track of a six-deck shoe. And, you know, make it look like I'm not keeping track because while counting cards isn't officially illegal, it is most definitely frowned upon and will get you kicked out and/ or banned if you're caught. I wasted another month fretting about the morality of counting cards because that's how autistically attached to rules and order I am. In the end, I somehow convinced myself that the attempt was within my acceptable boundaries, either because of some poorly articulated Robin Hood fantasy, or because it was for my big Autism Awareness cause. I don't recall exactly. I'm assuming I had completely lost the plot by that point in the half-assed project, anyway. By the time Vegas rolled around again, I hadn't even reached the actual counting part of my card-counting research. So I decided I'd spend that visit "observing."

The next year, I started by asking my therapist, who specializes in autistic adults, if he had any insight to add to my experiment. I had actual real-life problems that probably needed attention in that chunk of my not-exactly-cheap hour, but I just really needed to know. "I think I've figured out just how much I'm going to suck at the social aspect. I've been reading message boards on blackjack etiquette," I informed him. "But I was wondering what other factors you, as a professional, think might contribute to my inability to actually do this?"

He listed a number of environmental factors that were likely to overstimulate me or throw me off in some way, including the casino lighting, air fresheners, the buzz of the sound system and the crowds. "Remember, these places are designed to throw neurotypical people off and prevent them from focusing and making sound decisions. Given that you're more sensitive to these things in general, you might be at a higher risk for sensory overload," he concluded before begging me, not for the first or last time, to please stop treating message boards like a valuable insight into the normal people condition. That year, I went and observed the tables and all of the potential sensory traps, took a free blackjack lesson at the Golden Nugget one morning ... and concluded that maybe I would try an empty table the year after.

On our next trip—year three of the Rain Woman experiment—I spotted a free table in a quiet downtown casino, nervously plunked down a twenty and babbled something about being new, awkward and terrified. A very friendly and patient dealer and pit boss walked me through the process. The dealer and I chatted amiably about our hometowns, and I very slowly waded through a few decent hands. Then I got confused and made a weird basic strategy-flouting mistake that luckily ended up working out for me in the end. "If there had been anyone else here, they would have lost their minds over that," the pit boss pleasantly laughed. I cashed out five dollars up and confirmed that I would probably never risk more than that. Forget keeping track of the ebb and flow of six decks' worth of cards while playing; I couldn't add the mostly single-digit numbers on the cards in front of me while keeping up with the lowest stakes small talk! That was the end of my blackjack career.

When I returned home, I got an even more questionable idea into my head: I was finally going to watch *Rain Man*! I'm not even going to pretend that I went into this venture without bias. I fully expected to hate it. What I hadn't anticipated, though, was that I would be wounded by it.

This film has such an overbearing, lingering presence in so many autistic people's lives, and yet we have no actual presence in it at all. We weren't even in its conception. Kim Peek, the man who originally inspired the Raymond character, was a savant, but he wasn't on the spectrum. The whole autism thing was only shoehorned in because Dustin Hoffman had worked with some autistic people and felt inspired. We're not really present in the plot, either. Tom Cruise's Charlie Babbitt is the main character. It's his story that audiences are supposed to follow and care about. He's the one viewers are supposed to identify with. Raymond has no narrative arc or character development, or even any real hints of internal life of his own. He's there to make Charlie—and, by extension, the viewer—think, feel and grow. Autism was a whim or creative exercise for the talent, a device for the characters and an object for the audience. And yet it has defined the ways in which people perceive us and mock us ever since it came out. It's contributed to the stereotypes that have prevented autistic people who aren't like Raymond from being recognized, being diagnosed and receiving support.

I'm sure professional jealousy plays a role in my distaste for *Rain Man*. I have so many stories I want to tell, and I'd kill for a fraction of the budget that director Barry Levinson and company had to produce that film—or a tiny chunk of their audience. It runs deeper than that, though.

Before I knew who or what I was, before I even knew of *Rain Man* or autism, I knew that I was different. That I was something not like anyone else I'd encountered and therefore not wanted in the same way that the other people around me seemed to be. But I also started telling stories before I could even read them for myself, and I realized that they seemed to interest people. So I kept telling them, both because I enjoyed the act of doing so and because I hoped that maybe it might redeem me in some way. Maybe the stories could be a bridge, a way for me to connect with other people.

I learned so much about the world outside of myself from the books, music, shows and films I loved, and I thought maybe I could make the reverse true for that outside world and whatever was going on inside of me. And, just maybe, if they liked the stories, people might also learn to like me someday. As my employment prospects have faded, making a modicum of money off of my writing has also become the only real hope I have for staying afloat—and the only hope I have of ever being able to pay back the loved ones who have helped me so much along the way.

So maybe I am a frustrated artist seething at taller poppies, but I'm also a heartbroken human who feels lonelier every time I see another example of how the only thing I've ever been good at still isn't what other people want from me. That it's only embraced when people who aren't like me create fake mes and share them with each other. That it was never a bridge at all, but another way for them to close ranks. Watching non-autistic people get all of the glory for writing and realizing autistic stories without us—and finding more success than any of us who try to tell our own stories—stings. Knowing that other people will love the idea of you as seen through each other's eyes in a way that they will never love actual you *aches*.

And with every passing year, I feel the hope that things might change—for me or for anyone—slip away just a little more.

I've always felt like I was running out of time. Two days before my seventh birthday, my parents found me hiding by a closet and sobbing because I couldn't bear the idea of not being six anymore. I spent the bulk of my early-twenties two a.m.s almost breathless with the fear that my career—and my life—would be over if I didn't publish a book immediately. These episodes are ceasing to grow into cute anecdotes as time passes, though. The fears aren't things I can laugh or shake off as easily once the moment of panic passes.

There's a reason why this panic keeps resurfacing in my mind and in my prose. I *don't* have forever to achieve what I want to in life ... or anything at all, really. There is most likely going to come a time when my desires for my stories shift from a weakening but still resilient hope for a better future into a faded pipe dream. I don't have all the time in the world to make up for whatever mistakes and missteps I've made along the way. I will probably outlive not just my dreams, but the skills I have to make them in any way possible. And I will probably outlive the people who make that possible— hell, who make my life at all possible—too. Probably before I can ever properly thank them or even begin to reciprocate everything they've done for me and meant to me.

I was first confronted with the true brunt of this brutal reality in Las Vegas. Just a few days before my one and only blackjack experiment.

"You know, it's weird," I obliviously mused to my mom shortly before it happened. "I love this place so much. I have so much fun here, and yet I always feel like I'm the verge of tears!"

I don't know why it didn't occur to me at the time that it was probably anxiety. Maybe I was having too much fun to notice—or maybe I didn't want to admit it to myself. I was fully aware that my Vegas adventures had always been tempered with a touch of misery. They started with heatstrokes, lost luggage and meltdowns. I had a mild seizure at a bar shortly before the third visit. Given the correlation between epilepsy and autism, I figured I should immediately book an appointment with a neurologist to see what was going on. I was still in the middle of testing when it was trip time, so my therapist sent me down with a list of potentially triggering lights and patterns to watch out for. And I spent a week trying to avoid those things. *In Las Vegas.* Because no two people can live in perfect harmony in close quarters and without sleep for over a week at a time, Mom and I also averaged about one moderate but easily repairable argument per trip.

Whether I was distracted by these more obvious issues, or simply had my awareness dulled by cocktails, sleep deprivation or that mythic "casino air," I never noticed or considered what else might be happening to me while I was there. It hadn't consciously occurred to me that a place that flaunts its unceasing sensory overload as a selling point had the potential to become a bit too much for my autistic brain and body to handle at some point.

While my subconscious was doing its best to sidestep the panic squeezing at my tear ducts and throbbing in my throat and chest faster than any DJ set at a Vegas nightclub, there was something else brewing that my conscious couldn't ignore quite so easily. I was becoming more sensitive to touch. More specifically, I was becoming painfully sensitive to the way my mom lightly grabbed my forearm in nerves, excitement or just general fondness. This was new. It came out of nowhere. For thirty-four years, I had either not registered this gesture or found it a comfort, and now my whole body tensed in the very anticipation of it happening again.

I should have told her. I have no doubt that she would have been receptive to an explanation. My problem was that I was struggling to explain it—no, admit it—to myself. I was afraid of the future on the best of days. I hated change, and here I was changing. And I couldn't shake the feeling that it wasn't for the better. I could barely handle my life as is. What the shit was I going to do if it got more challenging and I became less equipped to face it? So I tried to ignore it, or at least ride it out, subtly trying to keep a little more distance between us when we were walking, shifting my arm out of reach if we were sitting next to each other at slots or on the bus, and gently pulling away when I sensed her starting to reach for me. Which worked until I was too exhausted and overwhelmed to keep it subtle or gentle.

I don't know when she started noticing it, but I'll never forget when she first mentioned it. Somewhere in the middle of Fremont Street, she pointed at something with one arm and reached toward me with the other. And my entire body jerked away from her. "I can't even touch you now?" she asked. Even if I'm still not perfect at recognizing tone, I can tell when a voice is breaking.

We stumbled through a circular argument on the way back to our hotel. Why hadn't I told her? I didn't know how. Did I really think she wouldn't understand? *I* didn't understand, how the fuck was anyone else going to? Was it really that bad? Maybe. I didn't know what was going on. Couldn't I imagine how hurt she was? Couldn't she imagine how scared I was? But we were both too tired, too wounded and too terrified in our own ways to make much sense out of what the other was trying to say or much progress with each other. She went back to the casino. I retired to the bathroom.

Somewhere out on that casino floor, a mother faced her worst fear: losing her only child. Maybe not losing her in the most permanent sense, but her becoming almost as unreachable. After every bit of love, and patience, and (over?) protective mama bear-ness, after every hour spent encouraging her, and helping her through her tears and triumphs, every concert and every vacation, every slipped twenty when her job couldn't cover her bills, and every treated meal and indulgence, her daughter couldn't even bear her touch? Like she was that loathsome? How could she throw her away like that?

That's the story that inspires sympathy. That's the one that would win audiences' hearts and awards. And I'm not saying that it's not powerful, or important, or valid. I'm not saying it doesn't shatter my heart to think about it. I just want you to know that, while that was unfolding, this other story was happening, too.

For a while, I sat on the bathroom floor, my head resting— okay, banging—against the door. There was only the sound of that thump, the lights and my erratic breathing as I tried to quell the frantic sobs. Then there was only the dull ache in the back of my skull, the much sharper pang in my chest and the cool of the tile against my cheek. When I managed to collect myself a little, I grabbed my phone and curled up in the bathtub, pressing my spine along its curve. (In the midst of this gut- and soul-wrenching existential/personal crisis, I distinctly recall thinking "Oh ... so this is why cats like curling up in boxes! It's so soothing.") I called my husband and tried to articulate what had happened. And why it happened. And why it was the end of the fucking world.

The gist of that desperate call, delivered at increasingly higher pitches, in mile-a-minute gulps, was this: My mom's upset. She just took off. I've really fucked it up this time. I didn't mean to. I didn't know what else to do but ... well, apparently I'm hyper-sensitive to touch now? I don't know what's going on there. I'm really freaked out about it. What if this is a thing now? What if I can't let the people I love touch me anymore? Like, it's just normal stuff that I've always done. That we've always done. She was just resting her hand on my forearm. It's no big deal! Well, at least it used to be no big deal. But now it hurts. IT HURTS. And I don't understand why and I'm scared. So today, she reached out for me and

I freaked the fuck out and it hurt her and she asked why I didn't just tell her but I didn't tell her because *I don't know.* Because I don't know how to tell myself that my sensory issues are changing and getting worse, and I don't know what is going to happen to me as I get older and I'm afraid I'll lose everything I am right now. And then I'll lose everything I have right now and I'm not ready for this. I'm so scared. And my world is only going to get smaller from here. What do I do if I can't come here anymore? What do I do if I can't handle people anymore? What if I start recoiling at your touch? Are you going to leave me? I mean, you should leave me, you know you can do better, right? I don't want you resenting me, you've done more than any other man would. And I love you. And I'm sorry. And I'm scared. I don't want to hurt the people I love, but what if I can't stop myself? What if this is what I am now? And it just plays into every fucking fear I have because what if I do just keep getting worse? What if I can't keep up anymore? What if I am just a burden to all of you? What if I can't ever pay you back for everything you've given me? What if I just continue to suck the fucking life out of you? What if I am an empathy-free monster and what if I am just being selfish right now? I don't think I am, but I don't know. I wouldn't know if I was a selfish automaton with no awareness of other people's lives, would I? But I do know Mom's upset and I do hate myself for it and this is the last fucking thing I want in the world. She's the last fucking person I would ever want to hurt. She's done everything for me and now I can't even let her touch me? What if we never recover from this one? What if I can never make it up to her? What if I can never make up this fucking phone call to you? You all love me so much and I don't deserve it and I'm just so overwhelmed all of the fucking time. And I'm just so scared. I just can't shake the feeling that there's going to come a time when I can't pay my way in this world, in any way. What if I can't work enough to pay my bills? What if I can't keep my end of my relationships? I know you're supposed to hold on and there's people who love you and they'll be hurt if you're not here, and I don't want to die. But what am I supposed to do if I just don't contribute enough to earn my keep here? What if I don't deserve to be here anymore? And I'm scared.

Eventually my husband talked me down. I apologized for troubling him, thanked him obsessively and told him I loved him. (Even if I really didn't think I was worthy.) Mom reappeared in the room and suggested a quiet night out if and when I was up for it. I apologized profusely. She said there was nothing to forgive. I didn't agree, but I appreciated her grace all the same. We talked about it later, when we were both more up to the task, and we came to a genuine understanding. They have both assured me, as many times as I have asked, that it's okay now. And to them, I believe it is.

To me, it's not.

Mom and I have returned to Vegas a number of times since then. The touching issue, mercifully, hasn't. We've started going to wrestling shows together, and now she nervously grabs my forearm every time she's afraid that a performer might get hurt. Which is often. It's so endearing. I love it. I hope she never stops.

I still love Vegas, too. I hope it never stops, either. But the realization that it might not be the perfect recurring destination for someone who has such a fear of change and a need for permanence is getting harder for me to ignore. Each year when we go back, there's another landmark missing, or another haunt that we're visiting for the last time. I notice the changes in my skin in the hotel room mirror from year to year, and my shifting ability to cope with the bustle outside of it. Each of these places we love and revisit will be just another memory eventually, and so will we. At some point, these trips will end, whether it's a result of money, mortality, the decline of the American Empire, the apocalypse or apocalyptic climate change. I'll never see and do everything as many times as I want to, or as well as I want to. At some point, I'll run out of chances to get it right. Probably before I can even articulate what this "right" is.

But as long as we can manage, we'll make the trip, and/or others like it. We'll enjoy the things we love and our time together. I'll do my best to recognize my changing needs and concerns and we'll both do a better job of finding ways to talk about them and make room for them. We'll have our weird annual spat and get over it. And we'll get what we can out of the time we have left.

I probably won't attempt blackjack again. I far prefer risking quarters on racing toy ponies and a couple of bucks on the most ridiculous slot machine themes I can find. I never did get a real thrill out of the act of playing cards or gambling itself. But I think I do get the appeal—or the compulsion—behind it now: that feeling that, no matter how far in the hole you are, maybe that next hand will change your luck. Maybe that next roll can finally start to recoup everything you've lost.

ACKNOWLEDGEMENTS

I AM WRETCHEDLY AFRAID THAT ACKNOWLEDGEMENTS ARE YET another non-autistic social convention that I will fail to execute properly. That I will do something weird with them that might put people off. That I might, in my overwhelming anxiety, forget to name someone, or not express my gratitude to everyone who kept me alive long enough to write this book—and then somehow kept me alive during the writing of it—strongly enough. And, worst of all, I worry that I might somehow inadvertently hurt someone I care deeply about in the process.

But I don't want to say nothing, either. So let's give this a try:

Mom and Dad. Aaron. My assistant, Arcadia. The Maddalenas, the D'Angelos, the Kurchaks, the DeVillers, the Brophys and all of the extended family not covered under these general banners. Scotty. Evan. Marty. Tara. Elisabeth and Sylvain. Kate. Natalka and co. Erik and Kristine and your wonderful families. Rachel and Brendan. Emily. Jorge and Suzy. Hannah, Shannon, Sofi and most of the *Chart* crew. Even you, Noah. The PFL fighters and extended family. Morgan. Krissy. Judy (not just for the amazing hair on the cover of this book, but definitely for that, too). Emily Brooks for the wisdom, friendship and Lulu Pencil fandom. Lulu Pencil for existing. Michael Shaughnessy, who has saved my fragile well-being more times than I've ever told him.

Any friend or family member I may have missed. You might be denied this moment in print, but you can exploit my guilt and desire to make it up to you for the rest of our lives. I hope that's a fair trade.

My agent, Stephanie Sinclair, who reached out to me because of an essay that Haley Cullingham published. An essay I never would have pitched if Nicole Chung hadn't reached out to me with vast amounts of encouragement and contacts. And every editor and cheerleader who got me to the point where this miraculous series of events could begin. Jess Zimmerman, who is both my favourite editor and one of my favourite people, period.

Anna Comfort O'Keeffe, Pam Robertson, Nicola Goshulak and everyone at Douglas and McIntyre for making this book a reality. Jenna Marie Wakani for putting my extremely anxious self at ease during the cover shoot—and making the final results as presentable as possible.

Everyone who thinks that following me on Twitter is a good idea, for whatever reason.

Everyone involved in DDT, for being my only source of joy during a taxing writing and editing process. ありがとうございました

Finally, to all of the autistic activists, advocates, journalists, Tweeters and people who are out there fighting for each other and yourselves to the best of your ability (and to our allies who often fly under the radar because part of what makes them great allies is that they don't hog the spotlight): thanks for putting in all of the tireless and often thankless work that you do. I put everything I could into this book—and it did its best to take so much more out of me—but it still feels like so little compared to what the rest of you are doing every single day. Thank you for your influence, wisdom, education, support and occasional bouts of commiseration.